HOLLYWOOD

UNDRESSED

OBSERVATIONS OF

SYLVIA

AS NOTED BY HER SECRETARY

BRENTANO'S
NEW YORK · 1931

~~~~~~

CONTENTS

Part Two

PART ONE

﹏﹏﹏﹏﹏﹏﹏﹏﹏﹏﹏﹏﹏﹏﹏﹏﹏﹏﹏﹏﹏﹏

I

THE WHAM WHAT AM!

JEAN HARLOW is in the back room, where Sylvia is giving her a spanking she'll remember—to judge by the howls. Three more of them are sitting around in the front room waiting their turns. The one who goes in next has already stripped and is sitting with a towel in her lap. Modesty? Modesty my eye! She's trying to hide her misplaced tonnage.

If we could save and market what the actor bunch of Hollywood comes into this massage parlor to have slapped off, we'd put Armour out of business. . . . Well, I've got to turn on the radio— loud. Those are my standing orders. Whenever

9

they begin to howl in the back room, cover up with music. I hunt over the dial until I get something with lots of static. . . . This tenor up in Oregon will do fine. There's jazz for you!

Wham! And listen to that baby howl! Sometimes—even though I've been with Sylvia a long time and I know they never die on the slab—sometimes I get scared and go in to see if the boss isn't getting too enthusiastic. . . .

I looked into the back room just now. I might have saved myself the trip. It's just the usual. Another talkie star (a moon, if you ask me!) is in there now, laid out face down on the slab, and Sylvia is going to take a pound of ham off her in the next fifteen minutes or know the reason why. Sylvia can do it, too. I've got to hand it to her. She's only four feet eight inches high and there isn't much meat on her—but what there is, it's all power.

She stands off about three feet from the target and winds up like a baseball pitcher. No need to take any special aim. This home plate is as big around as a balloon tire. When Sylvia lands it sounds like a pistol shot. That's because of the trick swat, reserved for the tough cases—the cases where the studio executives have gone into conference because the lady is bursting the seams in the gown for the ballroom scene.

That swat is something special. Sylvia cups her hand so that it shapes like a rubber suction pad, and when it lands it sticks for an instant and pulls away like a cork leaving a bottle. That's what fits them to their parts. The fat comes out through the pores like mashed potato through a colander.

Sylvia is working to the music ... *One* and two and *one* and two ... The victim goes *oof!* at each sock and cries like a baby in between. When she is through and limps away, she'll stop in the front room and hand over fifteen dollars for having been beaten silly.

I wish Sylvia would let me pinch-hit for her sometimes. On some of these motion-picture stars I'd do the job for nothing.

You gather that I'm not exactly sold on these

11

world-famous beauties of Hollywood who have been hanging their Paris underwear on our parlor lamp for the last four years at an average rate of sixteen a day. When you see sixteen motion-picture stars a day troop in and strip down to sixteen different kinds of physical results of overeating and other forms of self-indulgence, you get sour on the whole lot of them. You wonder how they get that way.

As I figure it, most of them never ate regular until they landed their first Hollywood contracts and now a menu just goes to their heads—their heads and their elsewheres. Eat, drink, and be stuffed, for tomorrow we may be fired.

The universal ailment is prosperity. In her date book, Sylvia has over a hundred film people catalogued according to the places on their physiques where their earnings show. They fall into one or more of five classes, one class for each place. There is such a thing as a film star who falls into all five. That's Marie Dressler. No wonder *... fourteen quarts of near-beer a day!*

OUR FIRST LADY STRIPS FOR ACTION

MARIE DRESSLER is the one woman whose name is in the date book as far back as 1925, who doesn't give me a pain. I guess everyone likes her. Even these cats that come in here with gastritis every time somebody else makes a hit in a picture can stand the idea that Marie Dressler is knocking them dead with every release. Maybe it's because Marie is nobody's rival for a beauty prize. What really burns them up is having some new cutie breeze into town hunting for a lap to climb on. Nobody got alarmed when Miss Dressler began squeezing through the doors of casting offices. And now it's too late to do anything about it.

The nightly prayer of the Hollywood female is: "Please, Lord, don't send us any more lookers." Heaven heard them once, and sent Marie Dressler.

Sylvia was giving Dressler her daily tumble before Hollywood ever did. Back in 1925, in "The Callahans and the Murphys," Dressler was just one of the supporting crowd—an aunt or something. Nevertheless, she was Sylvia's first movie client and her entering wedge into the film colony.

Yes, if Marie Dressler hadn't been loaded up with fourteen quarts of near-beer a day back in 1925, Sylvia might have gone back to Chicago. And me? I suppose I'd still be holding the towel for that dentist who couldn't pay my wages. But for Marie Dressler, Sylvia might never have hung on in Hollywood.

The boss told me about that first call to Marie Dressler's suite in the Ambassador Hotel. You see, in those days, being just a squarehead immigrant, Sylvia knew no more about the Hollywood film

14

world than you can find out walking down Vine Street at lunch hour, and reading the press blurbs. And what you see from that angle is all front— the big Hollywood front. It took her a couple of years to work around to the other side of Hollywood.

The call to attend Marie Dressler came quite unexpectedly. I don't need to say I wasn't yet on the scene. An unknown masseuse doesn't need a secretary to handle the appointment book and the collections. One of her patients was a Chicago woman visiting Los Angeles and staying in the Hotel Ambassador. This same woman was getting treatment by the hotel doctor, who was an A-No.1 M. D. and was on the level. So when Marie Dressler called the doc to her suite in the same hotel and showed him the symptoms of a gastritis, the doc recommended Sylvia.

And so Mae Murray and Alice White and Bebe Daniels and Mary Duncan and Ramon Novarro and Ronald Colman and Norma Shearer and Ruth Chatterton and Ann Harding and Norma

15

Talmadge and Grace Moore and Connie Bennett and Gloria Swanson followed in rapid succession, and today Sylvia stands at the top of her profession and has an electric refrigerator and a hired girl in the kitchen.

WELL, meanwhile, before going up to the Dressler suite, Sylvia stopped in to thank the hotel doctor for the boost. And she got to telling him how this was like a dream coming true——

"Because I worked a year in Chicago to save up enough money to come out to Hollywood," she told him. "I doped it out, doctor, that the one thing they want out here is to hang on to their good looks, which they can't do without some professional help. Now, this Marie Dressler—tell me confidentially, doctor. She isn't so sick, as she's afraid she has lost her shape or her complexion. Isn't that it?"

You see, Dressler was just a name to the boss, who hadn't been spending much money or time on the movies. The doctor got wise that Sylvia

16

thought she was to go to work on the alabaster surface of a piece of living Beverly Hills statuary.
He let it ride.

"The poor girl's a little overweight," is all he
said—with a poker face.

"Any bets I can't take it off?" said Sylvia.

"I'm not a betting man," he replied.

So Sylvia went on up to suite A3 to get her
first peek at Hollywood beauty languishing lux-
uriously in its lair.

As Sylvia tells it, she thought the girl's mother
let her in. As Marie Dressler tells it, a straw-blonde
midget came in through the letter slot, took one
look at Marie, and looked ready to cry. Sylvia
thought this was a put-up job, the doctor's little
joke.

The fact is, both were so surprised they could
hardly talk—Sylvia, to see a movie queen beyond
forty and over 160; Dressler, to see this half-size
visitor, the popular idea of a masseuse being
something like a big sister to a wrestling champ.

17

Dressler got her tongue back first. And Sylvia got her second surprise.

"What's your birthday?" snapped Dressler, looking at Sylvia the way she does—as if she saw where you'd hidden the spoons.

"April sixth," stammered Sylvia.

With that, another woman came rushing from the bedroom, pointed a finger at Sylvia, and challenged:

"Did you say April?"

Sylvia stuck to it, hoping it was a good answer. By now she saw what it was all about. The newcomer was an astrologer, and was already casting up a chart based on the April birth date. Dressler helped in the feverish scribbling. The other woman consulted a book and looked around at Sylvia with a violet-ray stare.

"Oliver Cromwell! Houdini! Nicholas Murray Butler!" She read the names off the page and, with each, gave Dressler a nudge. It seems these were people born under the same sign of the zodiac, or something, as Sylvia, and Dressler's

OUR FIRST LADY STRIPS FOR ACTION

astrologer friend finally gave Sylvia the okay as a masseuse. Personally, I can't see the connection. The only one in the list who would have made good in our line is Houdini. Imagine getting a facial · from Nicholas Murray Butler!

It seems Dressler never does much of anything without the okay of her star-gazer pal, who is Nella Webb, from New York. Seems Nella Webb told Dressler she could make good in the movies when Dressler was dying on her feet in New York theatrical agents' offices. Dressler laughed at the idea of selling herself in Hollywood, where anything old enough to sign its own contracts is a hag. But Nella Webb kept at Dressler until, finally, Marie took a last-chance ticket to Hollywood. The way I figure it, there must be something either to astrology or to Marie Dressler. One guess!

The first thing Dressler did when she got a contract was to move into the Ambassador suite. The second was to send for Nella Webb. It seems the astrology business in New York wasn't so strong at the time, and it's just like Dressler to get her hands on a ten-spot and then go hunting for somebody who needs five. Anyway, Nella Webb had just read her own stars, which said she was going to get a surprise. And Dressler is on the side of the stars. All the time Nella Webb was her guest, Marie Dressler spent half her time bally-hooing for her friend.

WELL, Neptune being favorable, Marie Dressler stripped. At that time Sylvia hadn't yet doped out her famous line with the movie stars. Today, when you come into our massaging room and strip for the slab, thinking maybe that, anyhow, your upper leg isn't so bad, Sylvia starts in diagnosing your defects out loud. Sylvia'd find something wrong with the Queen of Sheba. She has several reasons for taking this line with the Hollywood clients. For one thing, they love to be insulted. Then again, they insult you if you don't insult them first. And, anyway, Sylvia tells me she learned all her English from the Sunday comics.

But in 1925 she wasn't riding as high as she

is now, and she didn't tell Marie Dressler what
she thought of her figure. Maybe she thought something. But she didn't put it in words. Which, in the
circumstances, is a good example.

Dressler's trouble was swelling up around
that daily three gallons of near-beer. In the picture "The Callahans and the Murphys" she had a
scene where she was an old souse showing her
capacity. The director was one of these realists
and he set up a dozen steins of near-beer (stingy!)
for Marie to swallow before the camera. Then the
lighting was wrong or something and they had to
retake. It went on like that for a week—the same
twelve steins of slop to be engulfed daily.

"You could wring her out like a wash cloth,"
Sylvia told me.

In a few days, Sylvia had Dressler so that
she fitted around herself more comfortably, and
then she went to work in earnest to reduce and
beautify her. She began giving her facials—until,
one day, Dressler got off the slab and looked at

21

herself in the mirror. She looked back at Sylvia sort of mean.

"Look here, are you trying to improve my looks?" she demanded.

"Give me two more weeks," begged Sylvia.

"And I'll be ruined!" said Dressler. "Listen, I tried for years to get rid of this—and these— and these—and couldn't make it. Now, just as I find out that my fat is money in the bank, you come along and want to take it away from me. Scat!"

Since then Sylvia has been seeing Marie Dressler intermittently, the job being technically one of the most interesting she has. The idea is to leave a middle-aged lady in the comfortably cushioned state that nature intended. It's refreshing. All the rest of them want something they didn't get. They want to walk like a boy and throw a man's shadow. It's a novelty to meet a Hollywood female who is reconciled to the facts of life, one of which is that women and geese were made sidewheelers.

22

OUR FIRST LADY STRIPS FOR ACTION

SYLVIA was treating Dressler at the time of her great gamble. As Hollywood history goes, that was so far back that it's forgotten; but Dressler was out in the cold. After all the lean years that came before her first hit on the screen, it was tough to find herself "at liberty" once again. The studio didn't want to boost her price, and she got herself into a position where it was back down or quit. The old studio game: they sign you up on a sliding-scale contract that starts little and works up to auto-license figures—on paper. And then, when the date for the first raise comes around, they give you a song and dance about hard times, etc., etc. If it works—why not?

That's the way they figure. They didn't go into the dance with Dressler. In fact, they were still vamping for the song when she was a block away —through.

In those circumstances, most stars sell the new car and retreat back to New York. But Dressler is smarter than the average. She knew the bunch she was dealing with. What she did always works

—in Hollywood. She went out and rented a mansion in Hollywood Hills, got herself a second car (just a little Packard for the servants, my dear!) and laid in a winter's supplies and a high-priced Filipino chef to cook them.

That worried the studio, plenty. Looked like the holdout had some hidden assets. Both sides settled down to starve each other out. The studio had the money, but Marie had the nerve. She judged the situation to a nicety. On the very day when the money boys were standing around their front doors, sure that the next car would be Dressler's, bearing a repentant and humble actress, she made the win-all, lose-all move; she hopped on the east-bound express. . . .

They met her at Grand Central, holding contracts and fountain pens. They passed her the pen and said: "Sign here." For twice what she had been holding out for, of course. And it wasn't the hand that held the pen that trembled—no, sir, it was the hand that held out the contract.

24

∿∿∿∿∿∿∿∿∿∿∿∿∿∿∿∿∿∿∿∿∿∿∿∿∿∿∿∿∿∿

III

THE PRINCESS AND THE PEA

THE boss rubbed Marie Dressler and got a balance in the bank.

She rubbed others and got famous.

She rubbed still others and got wealthy.

She has rubbed some for charity, some on spec., lots for cash down—but, by and large, I guess she really rubs for the kick she gets out of her "art."

But the kick she got out of rubbing Mae Murray was different, and more than she bargained for.

It happened in the boss's earlier Hollywood

25

days. Mae summoned Sylvia about Christmas time, 1927, and spake:

"You come along with me on a coast-to-coast tour, and let's not talk dough. What you get by the week is—*poof!*—pin money. I've got *plans* for you. We'll launch a breakfast food! Say, we'll do better than that. When we get back, we'll open up a sanitarium right over in Westwood. There's millions in it!" And she got sentimental and added: "Think of your darling sons. Do it for them. They'll be rich!"

Now, I make a rule: When anybody says, "I know how to make a million," I'm deaf. If somebody says, "Want to pick up ten bucks?" I'm listening. But Sylvia is made different. She came home from the Mae Murray interview raving with enthusiasm.

I said right then: "This will end up in a lawsuit." That is exactly the way it did end up, and I got credit for second-sight.

Sylvia came back from the big tour with Murray minus salary she couldn't collect. So she sued.

26

THE PRINCESS AND THE PEA

Yes, they told it to the judge—but, your Honor, you don't know the half of it, dearie! The trial lasted two days, and they had it out in court—all about Mae's husband, Prince M'Divani, and his ways; about how Sylvia rubbed Mae so hard she got fallen arches (Sylvia did); about how Alice White was ready to show the judge just where Sylvia reduced her and there was a riot in court; and how one of Sylvia's lawyers told Mae not to throw any inkstands—all this was chewed over by the lawyers.

The boss won and collected.

The contract the boss made with Mae was to travel with her for six months from coast to coast and keep her in daily trim. When you've been dancing as many years as Mae the muscles of the legs begin to bunch up. All veteran dancers have this trouble. Most of them let nature take its course. But Mae is wiser. She can round into shape to this day and show a leg like a débutante's.

But Mae put it better than anybody else could in her testimony at the trial.

27

Sylvia's lawyer was trying to prove that the boss had had a hard time of it on the job.

(File No. 250,490, Los Angeles Hall of Records: in the matter of Sylvia vs. Murray: Deposition of the defendant)

Question (by Mr. C. M. Addison, for Sylvia). She neglected you, did she?

Answer (by Miss Murray). She was completely tired out many times, and went to her room without attending me.

Q. Probably true, because sometimes she gave you attention three or four hours at a stretch, didn't she?

A. No.

Q. Well, she did what you asked?

A. No.

Q. What did you ask of her that she didn't do?

A. Well, it was her complete attitude. The reason you have a masseuse is because you need it, just as a horse needs it when he's in a race. I'm in

28

a race four or five times a day. In dancing, your muscles become tired after twelve hours' work.

BUT the way to get it all straight is to start from the beginning—the day when we loaded the boss and Mae and all Mae's bundles on the train for San Francisco.

Outside a little fussing, all went like an Irish picnic until real trouble started to boil and bubble in the East.

Mae and Sylvia had reached New York by this time. Every few days along the road, Prince M'Divani, Mae's husband, turned up for a short visit. He is a tall, broad dragoon of a man who took a dislike to Sylvia. As near as Sylvia could make out, it was considered improper for a princess like Mae to get so intimate with the peasantry.

Meanwhile, there had been much discussion of the grand things Mae intended to do for Sylvia when the tour was over. The classy Westwood sanitarium for movie actors was more or less given up

29

by this time. "It might not work so well, after all," opined Mae.

But she had something much better in mind. It was a breakfast food. Mae was in correspondence with a Los Angeles food faddist who had got up a new kind of health food that was sure to be a rage. Just before Mae had left Los Angeles, the health expert had turned up on the railway-station platform with a crate of the stuff, and the cans of it had to be stowed away in Mae's luggage.

Now, in New York, Mae decided to look into those cans and give the food a try. Sylvia pried the top off a can and peered dubiously at the contents. The food looked something like that "wood paste" that you use for stopping up knot holes in furniture.

"I'm not hungry," announced Sylvia.

But Mae was made of sterner stuff. She smelled of the mess. "You're my dietitian," she argued. "You ought to test it."

"If I'm your dietitian and you're going to

take my orders," said Sylvia, "then I decide, let's dump it down the plumbing."

But Mae wouldn't agree to that. When she saw that nothing would induce Sylvia to take a mouthful, she did it herself. Well, she might just as well have taken Sylvia's advice in the first place. She took it now fast enough.

About this time it got to be Christmas again and Mae was due to open in Christmas week in a Buffalo theater. She had a brand-new vaudeville act. Under stage lights she looked slim and gorgeous. But she wasn't feeling as good as she looked. The reason was some disagreement with Prince M'Divani about what kind of Christmas present he should send his kid. The argument was still going on when the whole troupe got on the train for Buffalo. The prince decided at the last minute to come along.

Sylvia got shunted out of Mae's stateroom to make room for the prince, and the couple locked themselves in to finish that Christmas-money argument.

31

On the subject of that hectic first day and night in Buffalo the testimony of the trial of Sylvia's suit against Mae throws some little light:

(Sylvia vs. Murray: Deposition of the Defendant)

Q. Isn't it a fact that you paid Sylvia $275 the first week in Buffalo? [This sum was $25 more than Sylvia's salary.]

A. I don't remember.

Q. Wasn't it a fact that you paid her $275 at that time because you had got $25 in cash from her?

A. No.

Q. You say that Sylvia did not give you back $25 in New York shortly after Christmas?

A. Why on earth would I want to get $25 from anyone when I made thousands?

Q. Did you ask her for this money to give to Prince M'Divani?

A. No, certainly not. Such a low-lifed thing!

AT one point, this kind of questioning got Mae

so exercised that she cried: "I don't think you are an attorney at all—don't be funny!" And it was at just such another point that Sylvia's lawyer, Addison, exclaimed:

"Don't throw any ink bottles!"

"I might throw more than that!" cried Mae, but her lawyers got her calmed down and the questioning went on.

Of course, the lawyer traced the whole course of the rumpus with Prince M'Divani as far as it concerned Sylvia and her relations with Mae. He had her riled up again when he got to asking about the hectic night in Buffalo when she and Sylvia rushed out of the Statler Hotel and went to another hotel. Sylvia's claim was that, if she had ever missed a day treating Mae, it was because Mae couldn't stand rubbing; and that, other times, she had to pass up the visit to the Murray suite because Prince M'Divani was up there storming about his little boy's Christmas present.

So the lawyer tried to get all this out of Mae.

Q. Now, Sylvia and the Prince, your husband, had some words in Buffalo, didn't they?
[Mae said, "No."]

Q. And your husband wasn't mad at Sylvia
about anything?

A. Certainly not. She's a masseuse and
only that. What business had my husband with
her?

Q. Did Sylvia make a remark about the
prince—and didn't you repeat the remark to
Prince M'Divani, and didn't he——

A. Oh, certainly not.

Q. And when you arrived at the Statler
Hotel, didn't he order her out of the room?

A. No.

Q. Well, didn't something take place that
made it necessary to call the police because of
difficulties between yourself, Prince M'Divani, and
Sylvia?

A. Certainly not. The idea! [And Mae stood
up and shouted.] The blackmail of this woman is
all I've had since my arrival in Los Angeles—but

34

that won't stop me from suing her. That is the only reason she's held me up to get this money.

Q. You *have* had some difficulty with her, then?

A. Only since I came back home. When I realized she was trying to get money without working for it—and she called up the newspapers with these horrible tales—then I realized what kind of woman she is! And I'll fight this suit to a finish.

Q. You had no difficulties with her before all this? [Mae said she had had none.] Now, tell me, didn't you leave the Statler that night and stop with Sylvia at another hotel, the Tower—under the names Mrs. and Miss Jennings?

A. No.

Commenting on which denial, Sylvia is apt to get apoplectic and cry: "I suppose I dreamed all that!"

~~~~~~

IV

XMASI "X" MARKS THE SPOT

According to Sylvia, when the company got to the Buffalo Statler, everybody went to their rooms and crawled into the hay and hung out the Don't Disturb sign. Sylvia was just dozing off when—wham!—there went the phone bell: Mae, calling for a treatment.

Murmuring fond benedictions on the head of her employer, Sylvia crawled into clothes, dipped her face in cold water, and went upstairs. She found the prince alone, and the cordial relations existing between the Caucasian knight and the Scandinavian pawn led to an enjoyable interval of about a half-hour during which no conversation was exchanged. After a long while the prince did address to Sylvia one of the rare sentences that he let fall in her direction.

"Are all American women crazy?" he demanded.

When Mae came in a few minutes later, she was the spark to the powder. Right away the boss could tell there was something up. Mae had been out gallivanting around in the zero weather, dressed in a skirt and sweater.

"You'll have pneumonia!" said Sylvia.

"I hope I get it double," said Mae and began to sniffle. Sylvia went to comfort her.

"Take your hands off my wife!" roared the prince. "And what's more, Sylvia, you're fired! Understand?"

Mae stuck out her chin under the prince's nose and said:

"Sylvia *isn't* fired. She stays!"

The prince glared at Sylvia, and she got on the other side of the bed. He looked as if he were going to take the obstacle in one jump, but

37

contented himself with giving the mattress a big kick and yelling:

"You get out or—or——"

Well, Mae got him quieted down and he consented to leave the room. The minute he was out, she bolted the door.

"What's it all about?" Sylvia inquired.

"Don't ask me!" groaned Mae. "It's still that fuss about his boy's Christmas present."

Well, if it was just a Russian version of the Yuletide spirit, Sylvia thought she could risk sticking around; so she began treating Mae, hoping to head off pneumonia. For the next hour the prince kept trying the locked door and growling through the keyhole every few minutes.

After a while Mae dozed off. There was no noise outside, and Sylvia, being all in and starved, phoned down for a meal. When the waiter brought up the order the prince was lying in wait in the hall, and Sylvia no sooner drew the bolt than he popped in.

By this time Sylvia was hardened, so she sat

and ate her lunch and looked on at the domestic
scene in comfort from a neutral corner. Mae woke
up, and they went at it hot and heavy, until Mae
said she'd go over to the prince's room, where they
could have it out without witnesses.

But she was back in ten minutes, and made
Sylvia promise she wouldn't leave her, day or
night.

It went on like that during the rest of the
afternoon and evening, and along about bedtime it
got a good deal worse.

In the end, Sylvia was too far out of patience
to remember what she owed to an employer and
a member of the old Tartar nobility, so she gave his
Highness her candid opinion of him.

The hotel's house manager was on the noisy
scene by that time. He was scandalized and, being
a good American, couldn't get over how Sylvia
had talked to a blue-blood.

"Remember," he almost wept, "after all,
you're addressing Prince M'Divani!"

With the manager as mediator, Mae and the

39

prince worked out a compromise that restored order. The prince was to let his wife go to another hotel for the night, but as security he was to hold on to her theatrical trunks until she came back!

The arrangement deprived Mae of most of her private wardrobe as well, as the prince locked himself in and she couldn't get to her luggage. However, she and Sylvia slipped out of the Statler. They ducked, half frozen, into the first hotel they came to—the Tower.

The next day Mae and her prince got together again, the M'Divani boy got the Christmas present, and Sylvia got merryell from two directions. Mae and the prince decided Sylvia was responsible for the whole thing.

But the boss managed to stick it out for the next few weeks. The troupe got to Chicago, where it was to play one week and then break up. After that Mae and Sylvia were to return to Hollywood.

THE last performance of the tour came around. There's a time-honored stage custom that the star of a show throws a dinner for the supporting cast after the last performance. For a week Mae had been worrying about that dinner. There were ten girls to feed.

Sylvia got to the theater in Chicago early on the night of the last show, and ran into Jean Pittsman, captain of the chorus. Jean buttonholed the boss and asked:

"Where is Miss Murray taking us to supper? The girls are pestering me to know."

The other girls swarmed out of their dressing rooms, all excited, and pumped Sylvia, too.

Mae swept in from the stage door about that time and heard the girls chattering about the supper. She gave them a big, radiant Madame Happiness smile and called out:

"Girls, I have a surprise for you. Wait around after the show!"

The girls almost gave her a cheer. Mae motioned to Sylvia to follow her into her dressing room. Once inside, she closed the door and said:

"Sylvia, I need your help."

41

"To order the supper?" said Sylvia, bright and eager.

"Well, sort of," said Mae. "I just had a grand idea about that supper on my way down in the taxi. I do so want to do something nice for those darling girls, and I know just what will do them the most good. They absolutely ruin their systems, eating the stuff they do."

"They haven't much to spend on eats," put in Sylvia.

"Exactly," approved Mae. "That's why I've thought up this idea for them. It'll teach them to eat well and yet economically."

Even then Sylvia didn't suspect what was coming, and was left gaping and speechless when Mae opened her bag, handed Sylvia her trunk keys, and said:

"What I want you to do is go and get together all those cans of health food!"

"Health food!" was all that Sylvia could say.

"Wasn't I foolish not to think of it before?" Mae went on happily. "You remember how to pre-

XMAS! "X" MARKS THE SPOT

pare it, don't you? Get some olive oil and about
three cans of the food and—oh, wait a minute."

She went over to the dressing table and undid
a big brown-paper package. Inside was a large
salad bowl.

"I borrowed it from the hotel. Mix the food
in it."

As Sylvia turned to go, Mae cautioned:

"Don't say a word to the girls. I want it to be
a surprise."

WELL, Sylvia didn't say anything. She carried out
Mae's instructions to the letter and mixed up plenty
of the oil and health food in the bowl.

The act ended. Mae took her bows and came
into the dressing room. She gave the mess in the
bowl an extra stir and sniffed it.

"Delicious!" she murmured. "And now, Sylvia, call the girls in."

Sylvia started off to obey, but Mae stopped
her.

"No, I'll go to them with it."

She picked up the bowl and went over to the chorus dressing room, Sylvia tagging along. Mae threw open the door of the girls' room.

"Girls," she said, like a lecturer, "I want to give you a little talk. It's about eating. I've given the subject of diet a good deal of thought. Madame Sylvia, here, has been teaching me a lot——"

Sylvia got behind the speaker and sent the girls a wink meaning: "Leave me out of this."

Mae went right on: "After investigating every kind of diet I've found the grandest health food in the world. Now——" And she presented the bowl with a flourish. "Now I want you girls to try this food and tell me what you think of it."

The girls sort of drifted up to look and sniff at the bowl. They were more amazed than anything else.

"It's something you eat?" inquired Jean Pittsman in a dazed way.

"As much as you want!" cried Mae. "If this isn't enough, there's more where it came from. And I'm going to give each girl a can to take with her."

There was what you might aptly call a stage wait as the girls stared at each other, and then Mae said:

"Don't mind me. Go ahead and eat."

Jeannie had the presence of mind to speak up. "Thank you, Miss Murray," she said gratefully.

A little girl, the youngest of the troupe, came up and took a spoonful of the mess and put it in her mouth. A second later she spat it out.

Mae looked at her, maybe a little sternly, and the kid got frightened and apologized:

"I'm sorry. It slipped."

Mae left, with dignity. Sylvia went with her.

The girls took one more look at the mess in the bowl after she was gone, and grabbed their raincoats to beat it over to the doughnut-and-coffee stand, as usual. Soon they could be heard trooping back from their quick lunch. They were all laughing uproariously. Mae listened with a pleased look.

"They loved it!" she breathed. Presently she rose and said: "Let's see what they're up to."

Sylvia opened the door and popped out first——

And took one step and fell over the salad bowl full of oiled health food, as she made a desperate pirouette to avoid putting her foot right into it. The girls were disappointed. They had meant the trap for somebody else—they didn't say whom.

THE rest of Sylvia's tour with Mae was a succession of squabbles over moneys due and unpaid. Everybody got home alive enough to go to law. This account may as well end up as the trial did— with the sensational appearance in court of Alice White.

When Alice had first come to Sylvia, she had been as nearly disgusting-looking as so cute a kid can get on a cream-puff-and-chocolate-candy diet. Sylvia had taken her in hand and whacked her into such shape that the first thing a director asked, when an Alice White picture script was submitted, was: "Where is the undressing scene?"

Alice was determined to be Sylvia's witness.

46

"I'll be there," she insisted, "and I'll bet that judge invites me to testify."

In the concluding minutes of the trial there was a sudden commotion at the door. Alice had dressed in a costume which showed about as much of her as the law would allow. And she had a corsage of sweet peas on what there was of a shoulder piece to her gown.

Well, those court attachés had never seen anything like it. They opened up an aisle and Alice came down front. Sievers, Sylvia's lawyer, rose to address the court.

"I don't know whether this is material and ethical or not," he said, waving at Alice, "but there has been insinuating testimony to the effect that Madame Sylvia is not expert in her profession, and we have an exhibit here in court in the person of Miss Alice White."

"Let's have a look at the exhibit," piped up Mr. Gilbert, the opposition lawyer.

The judge took a look at Alice and said:

"File the exhibit."

47

Well, the legal boys had a lot of their idea of fun. Mr. Sievers asked Alice:

"What is your business?"

"Motion-picture actress."

Q. How long have you been so engaged?

A. Over two years.

Q. Throughout that time, have you taken massage treatments?

Judge Burnell. What's the purpose of this?

Lawyer Sievers. It is intimated, your Honor, that Mae Murray claims Madame Sylvia was no good at her job.

Lawyer Gilbert. Well, I object that Miss White's testimony can't be anything but indefinite, because we all appreciate that she looks like somebody's good job, but how are we to discriminate between that part of the result which would be attributable to God and those parts attributable to the father, the mother, and the masseuse?

Judge Burnell. Those parties you mention have not been made parties to this action. Even if

48

they were, I doubt whether they would have had you as their lawyer.

Loud laughter in the court.

Judge Burnell went on: "Do you wish the exhibit marked for identification?"

Well, everybody was willing to do the marking, and Alice sort of hitched around in her chair as if to inquire what part of her they wanted to put the seal on.

The judge got gallant. He gave a bend toward Alice, who gave him the eye, and he said:

"Please call this witness back sometime when we have an action that is going to last longer."

And Alice got up and left, and everybody that wasn't nailed down got up and tagged after her—so there were only the lawyers and Sylvia around to hear the judgment in Sylvia's favor.

~~~~~~

V

THE GREAT POISON PLOT

Wнen Mary Duncan came along in 1928 and wanted to sign up for Sylvia's exclusive services for a half-year, we were all against it—except Sylvia herself. A contract to massage anyone morning, noon, and night is worse than getting married. After all, a woman's husband can get away from her some of the time. But a woman's personal masseuse dresses her, undresses her, soothes her to sleep, spanks her awake, and (if the contract includes dietary work, as with Mary Duncan it did) watches every bite of food that goes down her throat three times a day.

I always figured that the real trouble between

Mae Murray and the boss was that everlasting intimacy. They were bound to get sick of the sight of each other. It's bad enough, in this massage business, to have to see the world without shirt and without manners. The only thing that makes it bearable is the variety when the practice is general and consists of a dozen different patients a day.

All of which I said to Sylvia, and much more —but you can't do anything with a Norwegian.

The opposition, which was giving Sylvia the arguments why she should take up Mary Duncan's offer, was represented by Sophie Wachner, the dress designer at Fox Studios, where Miss Duncan was starring. Miss Wachner had her own reasons for wanting Sylvia to go to work on Duncan.

"I can't fit dresses to Mary any more on account of her hips," was the way Miss Wachner put it up to Sylvia. "So, do a fellow a favor, Sylvia, and fit Mary to the gowns."

It was a rush job. They were starting to shoot the silent picture called "Our Daily Bread." The great German director Murnau was in charge, and

Mary Duncan was doing the rôle of a city girl who marries a farmer and gets all messed up in some labor troubles about farm hands having nothing to look at but miles and miles of Oregon wheatfields—and you can't blame them, not after you've been on location in those same wheatfields for over a month. You never saw the picture? Sure you didn't. It was one of the last silents and it was finished just in time to get tossed into the wastebasket on account of the sound screen coming in.

Sylvia had a small part of the blame for the trouble Fox had with that picture. But that's part of the story.

Well, Sylvia went over to the Fox Studios and though she promised not to commit herself before she left, we all knew that she was crazy to go on location with Mary Duncan and we weren't surprised when she came home looking sheepish and with an ink stain on her finger, where she had held the pen that signed the contract.

It seems that Sophie Wachner did a job on Sylvia as soon as she got on the Fox lot. Took her

THE GREAT POISON PLOT

into the wardrobe department and showed her the
dresses Mary Duncan was wearing in the opening
shots, which they had been doing in the studio.
Well, Mary Duncan had been putting on an inch
a day around the middle, and those dresses had
been let out until the waistlines were as full of V's
as a backgammon board. Sophie Wachner was at
her wits' ends, and was tearing her hair.

In her dressing room, Mary Duncan was another picture of woe—and a reasonably attractive
one. From any average point of view, there was
nothing at all the matter with the girl. But the
camera's is not the average point of view. Somehow, a lens always adds ten or twenty pounds to
the truth. The result is that the movie girls have to
be actually underweight—considerably so. On the
other hand, they mustn't show bones. So the type
that is most readily selected for film work is the
small-boned girl, short of stature, on whose underlying skeleton even a small amount of meat looks
like a nice job of padding. And the small-boned
short girl is the very type most prone to develop

53

along the lines called buxom. Mary Miles Minter, whose misfortunes caused her to let go and become what nature willed, has turned out now a plump and roundish little person—typically the figure that the majority of Hollywood girls would be but for strenuous battling against the tendencies of nature.

So Mary Duncan was in nothing worse than blooming health—and yet the Fox people were frantic.

The arrangement was that Sylvia should accompany Mary immediately to Pendleton, Oregon, where Murnau and the rest of the huge company concerned in the production of "Our Daily Bread" were already quartered.

THE Mary Duncan party included Sylvia, a Sealyham pup named Topsy, Mary's hairdresser and maid, a gallon of mineral oil (ace-in-the-hole of all reducing diets), and Mary Duncan herself. The get-away at the railroad station was just too cute for anything. You know—all innocent flutter and flashlight powders. As was shown next morning, when the party was rushed off the train at an early hour, Mary had hurried her departure so much as to forget one important item of her apparel.

They were met at the train by location executives and a mob of Pendletonians dressed in cowboy outfits and riding their ponies. The town was in the throes of a county fair, and it had occurred to some bright press-agent mind to have Mary named queen of the rodeo. They had a pony with a gilt saddle ready at the station and, when Mary was told that she was expected to ride the horse up Main Street, she was game. A bunch of the leading citizens got to kidding with Sylvia and thought she'd be great for the comedy relief, so they rustled a pony for her, too. As it turned out, Mary was all the comic relief the party needed.

For she had scarcely taken her place at the head of the mounted line and started up the street between the lines of cheering citizens, when her pony took a fancy step and sent her somersaulting earthward. A lynx-eyed kid in the crowd was the first to see there was something missing. He set up a loud-speaker yell:

"Hey! What a queen! She ain't got on pants!"

It was too true.

Well, Pendleton's one of those great open spaces where nobility is as common as nickels. The Pendletonians take Womanhood seriously. Any other town I can think of would have taken up the urchin's discovery and added footnotes; but Pendleton, as one man, looked down at its boots and didn't see anything. Though you never can tell, when a man's wearing one of those ten-gallon hats.

Mary took the incident all in the day's work, and pulled the best line: "I don't know what the parade was supposed to boost, but I certainly turned it into an ad for Sylvia."

Arrangements for the company's welfare were first-class, as they always were in the days of the William Fox régime. Fox prided himself on treating the hired help right, in which he was unique. The general practice of the studios is to handle the salaried bunch rough and economical, because they are too scared of their jobs to squawk. Mary had a nice frame house on a hill at the edge of town. Down in the hollow at the foot of the hill was a group of bungalows where the other important people of the company were quartered. Murnau and his manservant took the one nearest to Mary's house.

Sylvia got the kitchen going the next day, and Mary Duncan's house set the best table in the colony. The popular notion is that a diet is something inedible; but the rush among the company members to get invited to Mary's table is proof that you don't necessarily eat junk when you're eating correctly. The rest of the actors were glad enough to horn in on meals that not only tasted okay but left them fit for the day's work. The work was strenuous. Murnau had come up to get some big epic shots of the Oregon wheatfields—stretches of rippling grain that extended as far as the horizon, and beyond, in every direction. Sometimes the troupe would have to ride ten or fifteen miles of a morning to get to the location selected by

Murnau for the day's shooting. And, once there, the cast would have to turn unfamiliar hands to the plow and harrow. Some of them had to go out hours ahead of the rest and take lessons running all the sorts of huge engines they use on those enormous grain ranches. At night they would come back starved, and Mary, who had a big heart, would bring as many of them to the table as could crowd around it.

Somehow, without any formal arrangement being made, Murnau came to be the star boarder at Mary's table. He had a chronic weakness, one of the mild kidney disorders, and he was eager to benefit by the dietary regulations under Sylvia's supervision of the kitchen.

In fact, he came over one night, found Sylvia alone, and began to give out a doleful spiel about his symptoms. She thought: hurray, extra money! —and took Murnau into a back room to give him a treatment. Well, one of those misunderstandings developed. Ask any doctor about this question of handing out professional advice and services for nothing. With masseuses it's the same thing. People don't seem to understand that massaging isn't a parlor trick. People who pay the grocer regularly every Saturday and who settle for their bridge lessons in advance think nothing of trying to get a little friendly rubbing out of Sylvia for nothing.

I wonder what would happen if you got Rockefeller over to dinner and took him out to the garage and said: "Oh, Mr. Rockefeller, do show us how you fill a gas tank!" It all comes to the same thing. Rockefeller and Sylvia both do their stuff for a living.

Well, the situation got more and more in need of clearing up as the days went by. First, Murnau had a few little rub-downs on the spurs of moments, as you might say—administered in the den in Mary's quarters whenever Sylvia had a few minutes to spare. Murnau began feeling pretty good, and it occurred to him that thorough treatments at regular hours would make him feel even better. How would it be if Sylvia got up an hour earlier every morning to run down to his cottage and give him a once-over?

Meanwhile the regular eating of Sylvia's diet-kitchen meals was also helping Murnau considerably, and he gave her a free recommendation: said he'd never felt better.

One night, after a hard day in the fields, Murnau was so tuckered out that he couldn't face the climb uphill to Mary's dinner table. But he didn't want to make a break in his diet habits, so he sent his man up to fetch him something from Sylvia's kitchen.

Sylvia swears that she had no guilt in what followed. It was all an unfortunate accident. The man reported that his master only wanted a bit of salad. Sylvia prepared the ingredients of the salad bowl: vegetables, seasoning, and the inevitable bottle of mineral oil. This neutral, non-fattening oil is an obligatory substitute for olive oil in all cases where there is a disorder of the digestive functions. However, it must be used in moderation, being a fairly efficient purge in larger quantities.

THE GREAT POISON PLOT

HAVING assembled the materials for Murnau's salad, Sylvia was called away. She had two assistants in the kitchen. Assistant Number One came along, saw the salad fixings, and, in the spirit of helpful coöperation, mixed the dressing, using the prescribed amount of mineral oil. She went about her business.

Assistant Number Two came along, saw the salad fixings, and, in the spirit of helpful coöperation, mixed the dressing, using the prescribed amount of mineral oil. She went about her business.

Sylvia returned, noticed her salad fixings, and, in the spirit of helpful coöperation, mixed the dressing, using the prescribed amount of mineral oil. She sent the salad down to Murnau.

Accounts of Murnau's sufferings the next day, when the company went forth to a distant location miles from help of any kind, painted a pitiful picture. Much to Sylvia's pained surprise, she was told that evening that he had openly accused her of doing it on purpose.

For a week Achilles sulked in his tent,

refusing to grace Mary Duncan's board with his presence. He was finally driven back by need. The condition precipitated by the overdose of mineral oil persisted, and he came for relief. Sylvia was bland and gracious. She was really sorry, she swears, about what had happened, and was eager to make amends. She counseled a forty-eight-hour régime of rice water, toast, and tea without cream or sugar.

"Can you beat it?" she reminiscently exclaims, when she recalls the effect of the advice on the patient. "He shook his fists and strode out of the room violently.

"He went to Mary Duncan and complained that I was certainly and provably trying to do him injury!"

According to reports, he made the complaint with a great and Prussian dignity. He thereafter "punished" Sylvia by eating in a sort of protesting and injured silence, decorated with intermittent glances of suspicion and distrust cast in her direction.

Meanwhile, Sylvia's labors had borne fruits

THE GREAT POISON PLOT

in the form of a noticeable reduction of Mary's waistline. Those fruits were sweet to Mary Duncan, but, as it developed, were lemons to the Fox directorate. The wandering troupe packed up and came home to the Hollywood lot. There remained but a few interiors to shoot—on the home stages. These were the final sequences, showing the city girl back in the surroundings in which she had started the picture. And you can easily see that she had to look like the girl who had started the picture—which Duncan didn't. Slim in waist and cheeks, she looked like a different girl.

Winnie Sheehan, stern and masterful executive of the Fox lot, saw the shots of Mary Duncan taken at the end of the picture, and nearly jumped through the ceiling when he compared them with the earlier takes. He sleuthed around the lot and heard the story of Mary Duncan's doings with a private masseuse. He summoned the star and ordered her to fire "that lemon squeezer" at once. The interview almost precipitated a break between Mary and the company. Mary rushed feverishly forth from the conference with Mr. Sheehan and rebelliously offered Sylvia a renewal, for one year, of the contract.

But Sylvia's return to Hollywood was followed by indications that, at last, she had definitely gone over the top as a successful masseuse, much in demand. She got sense at last and saw that the real money lay in giving treatments to all comers, charging what the traffic would bear.

〜〜〜〜〜〜〜〜〜〜〜〜〜〜〜〜〜〜〜〜〜〜〜〜〜〜〜

VI

NARSISSIES

Ramon Novarro was a little stiff.

Why shouldn't he be? He sleeps in a coffin.

That's a fact. Ramon's bedroom in the immense house he occupies with an old grandee of a Spanish father, his mother, and ten—count 'em—ten brothers—Ramon's bedroom is a replica of the burial crypt of some saint in the Vatican City in Rome. The bed itself, high, narrow, and set on a pedestal, is a sarcophagus, under a purple canopy crowned with a wreath of thorns. A funny idea, this. All I can say is that Ramon seems to want to hurry his Cecil B. De Millennium.

Sylvia says that the daily massage she gave
Ramon at 7 A.M.—waking him out of his embalmed
slumbers with the laying on of her hands—always
felt spooky. It was too uncomfortably like a
miracle.

The boss promoted the job with Novarro herself, one day when she had finished touching up
Elsie Janis and gone down into the Janis back yard
to see what was going on in the swimming pool.
Quite a bunch of actors were splashing about, showing off; and as Sylvia came along Ramon Novarro
dived in and came up floating on his back. Right
away the boss's eagle eye noted something that
promised a new customer and she thought up a
salesmanship scheme.

"Can you float like that indefinitely?" she
asked Novarro.

"As long as I want," he modestly asserted.

"While you smoke a cigarette?"

He lit up and puffed away, and was good for
ten minutes, stomach up, under a broiling Califor-
nia sun. Sure enough, when he puffed the last puff

and called Sylvia to witness that he had accomplished the feat, the nice round central part of him was dried by the sun, making a cute little dry island in the middle of his bathing suit where it had been raised above water level by an undeniable protuberance.

Neat, what? All Sylvia had to do was kid him about the watermark and he had to say the expected thing and invite her to undertake the removal of the island.

"How could I help it?" he alibied. "I'm just back from a trip to Germany—and who can resist Münchener beer?"

ERNEST TORRENCE is a contrast to the soft and delicate Ramon Novarro, but not such a tremendous one as you'd think. What I mean is, all the boys get girlish and skittish when they have to take a professional interest in their looks, and big Ernest is no exception.

Like all those oversize fellows, Ernest has a small, firm-minded wife who bosses him around as

67

if he were a young St. Bernard. Elsie Torrence had been taking treatments from Sylvia, and she reported that her husband was threatened with nervous breakdown and ought to let Sylvia treat him.

"But he's so shy," Mrs. Torrence said, "and he just has fits when I suggest that he call in a female masseuse." She set her jaw and added: "I'll bring him round, though."

So Sylvia wasn't surprised a few days later when she got a phone call from Mrs. Torrence, who whispered hoarsely: "Come right over. He's taking his bath and doesn't know what he's in for, but we'll handle him."

When Sylvia got over to the Torrences' cheerful and attractive English house in Hollywood, the big he-boss was still splashing around in the bath and Mrs. Torrence was waiting with her finger on her lips.

"You get all ready," she cautioned Sylvia, "and I'll go in and tell him his time has come."

Sylvia rolled up her sleeves and fixed up the bed for the operation. Meanwhile, whines of protest in a guttural masculine voice came from the other side of the bathroom door, and Sylvia heard the missus lecturing the big fellow until finally he ceased his objections, and the little woman came out and nodded to Sylvia that it was okay and maybe she had better be gentle the first time.

In a little while, red as a beet and so flustered he giggled between words, Torrence lurched into the room enveloped in a bath robe which he had tied about his coy person with a sailor's knot.

"Take it off," ordered Sylvia in the casual, business-like manner that usually puts the patients with an excessively shy-violet complex at their ease. But Ernest wanted Sylvia to handle him with his robe on.

"It's just a light robe," he urged. "It won't interfere."

"Take—it—off," repeated Sylvia, beginning to figure on having to use cave-woman methods.

Well, the trick knot in the robe cord gained Torrence some time and his bashful dodgings gained him some more, but in the end he had to get around to the unveiling. The robe fell to the floor and he stood forth in all the noble and stalwart dignity of a strong, statuesque male—securely done up around the middle with three bath towels held together with about a dozen safety pins.

Well, Mrs. Torrence and Sylvia just fell over and howled. But Ernest couldn't see that it was funny, and he almost revolted when, for the next five minutes, the two women, after laying him out on the bed, kept busy picking the pins out of the extemporized girdle. He wanted to wriggle away and make a dive for the chaste security of the bathroom; but the little wife said a few firm words, and he turned over and lay quiet.

The matter with him was pure nerves. He had been worrying about his career and some trouble about his next rôle, and had lashed himself into a state bordering on complete breakdown. There's a legend that men are tougher than women, and lots of men are ashamed to admit, even to themselves, that they sometimes get out of their depths in this tough business of living. The plain truth is that men are, if anything, more nervously fragile than women.

SOME of the Hollywood actors have no false masculine modesty, but frankly admit that they are professional beauties the same as any Norma Shearer, Clara Bow, or Greta Garbo. There was nothing coy about Jack Holt's summons to Sylvia to come and give him facials. His face was his fortune, madame, he said, and he was ready to invest in conserving that asset—or maybe I should say facet. Jack gave the boss a thrill by receiving her, for the facials, mind you, clad in bright purple silk underdrawers.

While she was treating patients in the Malibu Colony, Sylvia threw a jolt into Neil Hamilton one day that was not part of any treatment. Neil was living down in Actors' Row on Malibu Beach, where half the movie colony lives through the summers in a row of dinky shacks built on piling in the beach sands. Sylvia had quite a few patients in the beach colony, and she tried to save time by calling on all of them whenever she went down there. She just

71

went along the row like an iceman on his rounds, knocking at every door and inquiring, "Treatment today?"

One night she stayed late at Anna Q. Nilsson's shack, and was going to call it a day when she noticed a light in Hamilton's place, a few yards down, and thought it good business to turn her roadster into Neil's back yard.

She heard several men calling excitedly to one another inside the house and then all the lights went out. She got a panicky notion that there was something wrong and crashed into the shack without knocking. Inside all was darkness, and Sylvia got scared and let out a yell. She heard somebody stumble in from the kitchen and she caught Neil's voice calling:

"It's a dame. Come on out."

Then the lights went on, and Neil and several of his friends gathered around Sylvia and enjoyed some private joke they wouldn't let her in on. Nor would Neil ever explain, except to say mysteriously:

72

NARSISSIES

"Whatinell do you want to drive around in that kind of a roadster for?"

Sylvia could only guess at what frightened the party, but that night she did notice an item in her newspaper:

"A raiding squad of the Federal Prohibition unit has been equipped with four Chrysler roadsters to facilitate work in the outlying areas around Los Angeles. A drive to dry up suburban areas hitherto immune will be conducted by the automobile squad."

CAN'T kid Lawrence Tibbett, another of Sylvia's male patients, when he does it so well himself.

Tibbett heard the general report, spread around the Metro-Goldwyn-Mayer lot shortly after Grace Moore's arrival to play in a musical opposite him, that Sylvia had taken several inches off Grace's contours. He decided to get Sylvia to give him one of her great big hands. And the first thing he said was:

"I hear you spanked Grace into shape. Well,

73

HOLLYWOOD UNDRESSED

I need the same treatment, only at the other end of my spine."

And he pointed at his face—that odd round short face, the shape of which the directors disguise by giving him rôles as wild Tartars and other wearers of plenty of crazy hair—which the make-up men arrange around his face.

The name of Tibbett's forthcoming picture at the time was "New Moon." He kidded himself: "I don't want the wise-crackers saying, 'It isn't a new moon—it's a full one.'"

Tibbett fits right into the traditional picture of a musical virtuoso—a troubadour born out of his century. Give him his way and he'd be going around the landscape with a guitar on his back, singing in everybody's back yard.

A much-repeated anecdote around Hollywood is that Lawrence had such an irresistible yen to express himself one night that he just had to go out and find somebody to serenade. He picked on Laura Hope Crews, which makes this so respectable that it almost isn't an anecdote. Lawrence wheeled him-

74

self over to Laura's house, and ran his car up on
her lawn so as to throw the headlight on her bedroom window. And then he did a solo, accompany-
ing himself on the car's French horn.

Well, when Laura and the neighbors got over
their first fright, they saw who the singer was and
decided to enjoy it. Even the cop on the beat had
enough æsthetic sense to lay off. No harm done, and
a swell time had by all.

But Grace Tibbett, his wife, couldn't see it that
way. She expressed her opinion in no uncertain
terms. And what she resented and disapproved was
not that Lawrence should desert the connubial roof
at the witching hour of midnight to go and sing
into some other woman's shell-like ear. No, it wasn't
that. What Lawrence was guilty of was putting on a
show without collecting a cent at the gate.

In Sylvia's contact with Tibbett she ran up
against Mrs. Tibbett's attitude only once. That was
during the first treatment. The boss was sort of
counting on getting an eyeful of the famous Tibbett
physique. After all, when a manly chest and Greek

75

torso have been as much publicized as in the case of Tibbett, even a masseuse can figure on getting some kick out of a close-up. So Sylvia was all set to go over Lawrence from toe to scalp. But the wife popped in at the psychological moment:

"Just a facial, please." And just facials it was.

ᗰᗰᗰᗰᗰᗰᗰᗰᗰᗰᗰᗰᗰᗰᗰᗰᗰᗰᗰᗰ

VII

A GALLANT EPISODE

HERBERT BRENON fixed
it up for the boss to handle Ronald Colman, and
pretty near got Sylvia pinched.

Colman was living down in the Malibu Beach
colony. Malibu is about the most unprivate community in the world. In the first place, the match-
board shacks are built so close together that when
your neighbor takes off his shoes you call, "Come
in." But the movie people are used to getting in
each other's hair, and like it, all except Greta
Garbo, who tries to stick to her own toothbrush.
So the lateral propinquity, as you might call it, is
not a drawback in Malibu. But the longitudinal

propinquity—the nearness to sea water on the one side and an eternal automobile procession of fandom on the other side—sometimes creates trouble. You're always finding a snail or a tourist in your oatmeal.

About the time Sylvia went down to Malibu to look up Colman, there had just been an epidemic of peeping Toms and Thomasinas plaguing the colony. Of course, the ladies were bothered most. Fans with big goggle eyes on stems were emerging from behind the wall paper at all sorts of embarrassing moments. Believe it or not, film girls who would act in a De Mille production without thinking anything of it can get just as nervous as an Iowa schoolma'am about a funny scratching noise at the bathroom window.

But if you think it was only the girls that were bothered by peepers, you don't know fandom. Every morning there was just as much excitement about the size-five footprints outside the boys' windows as about the size-nines outside the girls'. The colony was all excited that Sunday morning when Sylvia reported at Colman's shack for duty.

The boss walked in without knocking and got held up by an alarmed Filipino.

"Go 'way, please," he squealed, and shook a towel at her.

"Where's Mr. Colman?" asked Sylvia with authority.

"In bed, please," protested the Filipino, and got in front of Ronald's door, where he prepared to die. "Go 'way, lady!" he kept squealing.

"In bed?" said Sylvia imperturbably. "Good. That's just where I want him. Let me by."

"No ladies allowed," quavered the Filipino, who was really frightened. "Be quiet! I call police!" And he got a desperate hold on the door knob of Ronald's door and began to bleat.

His cries were answered by two men who popped out of guest-room doors. Sylvia recognized them as William Powell and Philip Strange, two cronies of Ronald's. But they didn't know her at

79

all. Strange took charge of the situation in a calm, haughty British way.

"Come now, my good woman," he remonstrated. "Tell us what you want."

Sylvia got wise to what was eating them and amused herself by feeding their panic.

"I just want to rub Ronald Colman," she begged, trying to put a strange glitter in her eyes. "Just let me rub him once!"

"Oh, now, tut, tut!" soothed Strange.

The Filipino began again: "Go 'way, lady, go 'way!"

And Colman put a sleepy head out at the door to inquire what was wrong.

"The woman wants to rub you," Strange explained.

"Well, why not?" yawned Colman. "She's my masseuse."

Strutting into Ronald's chamber, Sylvia stole a backward glance at the nonplussed trio in the living room. She got a distinct impression that Philip

80

A GALLANT EPISODE

Strange bally well didn't approve of such goings-on.

The boss still counted Colman among her steady clients when she got mixed up in the series of errors that turned out to be comedy but might have been tragedy, and that established Constance Cummings, the Broadway ingénue, as a newcomer in the films.

A LOT has been reported about how Connie came out to be Colman's leading woman and got shelved. The boss was looking on while all that happened and thinks it's about time Connie's side of the tale was told.

Sam Goldwyn "discovered" Connie on Broadway and let out a yawp of triumph that reverberated clear across the country. A girl to play opposite Colman, who is Goldwyn's chief star, was badly needed—and Sam let the world know that the priceless jewel was found.

I'll leave it to you to imagine whether Connie was pleased or not. Maybe she was ditching a stage

81

career; maybe she wasn't. But she didn't put up
any terrible fight against taking the first train west
and maybe dripping a few press interviews at sta-
tions along the line. In fact, Connie took the movie
offer to play opposite Colman as anybody else
would: went home and kicked a few chandeliers,
yelled to ma to put on her rubbers and hat, and
ran to Grand Central Station because taxis lose so
much time at crossing stops.

It was too good to be true, and she kept pinching herself all the way across the country. The
dream lasted until she got to the United Artists lot,
on to a sound stage opposite Colman, before the
test camera and mike. And then——!

What happened was that the tests established
that Connie, a husky, solid lass, showed up what is
Colman's most pronounced defect as a movie hero.
The handsome English actor is too delicately
modeled. He has ankles and wrists almost like a
high-school girl's, and a general pronounced grace
of build. To dissemble this fact, it is necessary to
surround Ronald with the most fragile and petite

A GALLANT EPISODE

feminine players, who can make his frame seem
sturdy by contrast. The strips of film taken of
Connie playing scene bits opposite Ronald left an
impression that his new leading woman could pick
him up and juggle him.

Goldwyn's staff got around the infallible im-
presario and shook heads and intimated that for
once he had guessed wrong. Then the problem
arose: how to inform the public that a mistake had
been made. Announce that Ronald was too small
for his leading woman? Unthinkable! Admit that
Sam Goldwyn had gummed up the works? What!—
Sam?

They sized up Connie and guessed, shrewdly
enough, that they were dealing with that rarity
among women, a good sport. They took a chance
and sent out a curt announcement: the newcomer
was "not suitable." The things that are hinted by
"not suitable"! Bowlegs, a bass voice, curvature of
the spine, cross-eyes, harelip. In this charitable
community the Goldwyn announcement was sure to
be interpreted to mean all this, plus a slight touch

of senile decay. And the Goldwyn staff darn well knew it. But there were two quivering masculine sensibilities to be spared—million-dollar sensibilities, too, whereas Connie's was only a five-hundred-a-week sensibility.

The girl was crushed.

As she sobbed it out to Sylvia: "I got to thinking maybe I *was* all wrong. I looked in the mirror and what I saw looked like a hag. That's what suggestion can do to you."

She had been coming to Sylvia before the blow fell, and she flew to our back room and locked herself in there with the boss to bawl about the bad news.

"Why don't you spill your side?" urged Sylvia.

"No." Connie shook her head. "That wouldn't be square."

She wanted to put on three veils and sneak down and take a night train back to New York; but Sylvia wouldn't let her.

"And if it's a stake you need—" the boss offered. But it wasn't that. What was eating Connie was the humiliation and the prospect of having to make long explanations to all the busybodies, without feeling free to give the true one.

Well, the boss was right. Cummings hung around, and, sure enough, Harry Cohen over at Columbia grabbed her and put her in "Criminal Code."

Anybody can get Sam Goldwyn's goat these days by just whispering three words: "Not suitable, hey?"

~~~~~~

VIII

HIGH HAT

Philosophical observation: There comes a time in most lives when you begin to step on the gas; you make speed; also, you bounce!

Sylvia began bouncing the minute she went under contract to Pathé and began working on the sacred cows that were grazing on that lot. Dough, dough! But also trouble, trouble! Ooh, lots of trouble. In fact, Sylvia got hooked up professionally with all four of the following at once: Gloria Swanson, Ina Claire, Grace Moore, and Constance Bennett.

There's a quartet for you! Maybe there'd be a

fight if it was said flatly that those four were at the top of the Hollywood heap. There's room for argument, with Greta Garbo left out—and Marlene Dietrich, and—oh well, write your own ticket. But nobody is going to dispute the statement that, in their own estimations, they are.

There was a queen of antiquity who used to protect her standing as the most beautiful woman in the world by a simple device. If any of the other lookers inside her borders got possession of some beauty secret, she would call out the head executioner and pay the rival a little call having for object a funeral and confiscation of the beauty preparation.

Since Cleopatra's day things have changed. Less cutting off of heads, but more beauty preparations. It has made the career of the professional beauty much tougher. It was a lot simpler, maintaining supremacy by killing off the competition. It's got so tough nowadays that a Queen of Beauty actually has to be beautiful. Not only that, but she has to stay that way. When you figure that, if left

87

to her own and nature's devices, a woman stays at the top of her form only about three or four years (and those usually the years when nobody but her school-teachers and the neighbors' boys are giving her a tumble), you can see what she's up against. By the time her photographs are beginning to appear in the silver frames in jewelers' windows, she doesn't look like them any more.

The professional beauty has to watch two angles: building up her rep, and living up to it when she's got it. I'll say one thing for the girls that claw their way to the top. Though they have their press agents to pull them and their beauty experts to push them, they do most of the work themselves. Being on the inside, where they are pulling all the strings and going through all the contortions of their beauty jobs—that's excitement! To be behind the scenes and watch them feint, grab, and foul when the referee isn't looking—that's high comedy!

The opening scene of a sample of it is the Pasadena station of the Santa Fe Railway, with the

Chicago-New York train due in any minute. Choo-choo. Toot-toot. A general rush of press agents, cameramen, Pathé executives, porters, dogs, and dust. Who is this stranger who trips as lightly as may be from the drawing-room car?

It is Ina Claire. Look out, Hollywood!

THE famous Broadway actress came to Hollywood with a chip on her shoulder. They usually do. When they've been here a while—they get another chip and wear them symmetrically, one on each shoulder.

The boss had her first glimpse of the Eastern invader a short while later, after Ina had reported to the Pathé lot for work in her first sound movie, "The Awful Truth." A three-alarm went out for Sylvia after the first test shots. Avoirdupois.

Hedda Hopper, our old reliable booster, was the messenger. She was on the phone with the S O S: "Ina Claire has to be taken down ten pounds in three days. Come and do it!"

Sylvia had seen Ina some years before in "The

89

Gold Diggers," when, if anything, the girl was a little too slim. So when she reported at Ina's suite in the Beverly-Wilshire and was inducted into the bedroom, she gasped in amazement. A voluptuous creature, very different from the slim Broadway star of yesterday, was taking her ease in a bed heaped up, à la French boudoir, with about a dozen small comfort pillows. Swimming in linen and lace, the star was probably supposed to be a study of beauty at rest. She was all of that. In a word, she was visibly overweight.

Grouped about the massive royal bedstead were the various ministrants to the lady's luxurious ease—maids, more maids, a secretary. The idea seemed to be to spare Miss Claire the exertion of lifting an arm.

What Claire wanted (and at first they're all the same in this respect) was for Sylvia to go to work, not too painfully, mind! and give her a ten-minute absolution for all past sins of overeating and insufficient exercise.

The boss sized her new patient up. Irish—

which means a good-sized bump of competitiveness. The line to take with her was obvious. As Sylvia pounded and slapped, she casually named a few of her other patients: Alice White, Norma Shearer, Ruth Chatterton, etc. Between grunts, Ina raised a face on the surface of which was faintly detectable an expression of awakened interest. What about them?

"Well," said the boss, "they're all out doing their morning conditioning work right now——"

At that moment a maid entered with a large frilly tray loaded with a huge breakfast. Sylvia glanced at the horrible display and significantly added:

"—*after* taking a breakfast of orange juice."

For one so far gone in the ways of comfort, Ina was quick on the trigger. Hitherto she had been taking Sylvia's line of nasty hints (hints that are about as subtle as a blackjack) pretty tartly—with a few cracks meant to convey the idea: "You get your pay for putting me in shape; go ahead, and don't annoy me with any remarks." But now, all of

91

a sudden, she got the point—quicker than do a lot of newcomers—and she sent the maid away with the breakfast tray.

And she was forthright enough to admit, a week or so later:

"I guess I took the wrong tack with you at first, didn't I, Sylvia?"

That gave the boss an opening, and she came out with a thing that was being said around town about the newcomer: "She's high-hat." Than which there can be no more final and dooming verdict by the Hollywood jury.

"Well," said Ina in a confidential tone, "I'll tell you: I was told to be high-hat when I left New York. People supposed to know came around with advice when they heard I had a picture contract. They said: 'Spit on them out there. They like it.'"

From then on, Ina began to alter her manner toward the film colony. Not immediately, but by slow degrees. Before she got entirely over her first notion that Hollywood had to be handled like a night-club waiter, she had one famous run-in with one of her competitors.

She wanted Sylvia to report every morning at 6 A.M. and wake her up with a good pounding. But Sylvia was already booked for that hour, Alice White having had the same idea about a six-o'clock slapping before it struck Ina as a good one.

"Tell Alice White," said Ina in all seriousness to Sylvia, "that if she'll give up the six-to-seven hour I'll——"

And she paused dramatically.

With her practical mind, the boss said: "You mean, you'll pay her?"

"Pay her!" Ina nodded and struck a pose. "I'll pay her with something more valuable than money. Tell her I'll *give her stage lessons!*"

Alice White's reaction to the generous offer was not long in getting itself spoken: "You tell *her* that I don't need drama lessons as badly as she needs lessons in how to move around in front of the camera without showing too many of her profiles!"

This little loving exchange between sisters-in-

93

art would have remained a private conversation but for one thing. Alice Glaser, then the wife of Barney Glaser the scenarist, was a chum of both and, hearing of the incident, couldn't resist telling a newspaper man about it.

Incidentally, the leak of the anecdote into public print caused a quarrel that flowed and ebbed for several months, until it resulted in a redistribution of mutual esteem. Ina took her intimates to task, one by one, seeking to find out which had betrayed her to the press. Alice blamed Sylvia and Sylvia blamed Alice, and it went on that way, back and forth, for a long while, until finally Mrs. Glaser, just to show Sylvia where she got off, quit taking massage treatments from the midget viking.

∧∧∧∧∧∧∧∧∧∧∧∧∧∧∧∧∧∧∧∧∧∧∧∧∧∧∧∧∧∧∧∧∧∧∧∧

IX

HER WEDDING NIGHT

To GET back to Ina: She moved presently into a house in Beverly Hills and, about the same time, began to be rushed by Jack Gilbert.

Jack, one day, called Ina "boyish," meaning it as a compliment—meaning that a tomboy was to his taste. Right away, Ina began to worry a bit—because Jack's calling her a tomboy didn't prove anything except that he was maybe nearsighted. True, she had square shoulders and a husky, boyish voice, but at the time she was wearing a few curves that were about as masculine as a bustle. And sooner or later Jack was bound to watch her going

95

up some stairs or something and wonder what on earth had ever made him think she resembled a boy. But a woman in love isn't stopped by anything so temporary as a fact. Ina had a heart-to-heart talk with Sylvia and said she didn't care how much it hurt, she wanted to be spanked loose from about ten pounds of accumulated femininity.

In a little while, Ina's campaign developed to a point where she decided for a shown-down. And she selected a certain evening as the zero hour. On that evening there was to be a big masquerade ball given by Basil Rathbone and Ouida Bergere in the Beverly Hotel. And Ina decided to go as a boy.

For a week she conferred and argued with the costumer, until a costume, consisting of form-fitting pink velvet pants and a boyish blouse, was settled on. And Ina was still, after several weeks of violent massage, frankly feminine and hippy.

With tears in her eyes, she begged the boss to go to it, to double, to triple her fury—to do anything, just so Ina could go to that party with the silhouette of a boy.

96

Sylvia gave a characteristic answer: "Tell that costumer to make the size of pants you want to wear. Tell him he doesn't need to fit the pants to you. I'll fit you to the pants."

Well, in the next five days Sylvia delivered a flank attack that Ina won't forget in a hurry. Ina never whimpered. Ah, love! What sufferings we support in thy name! If some artist wants to substitute a modern idea for the old one of Cupid letting fly an arrow at Beauty's heart, let him draw a pint-size Norwegian straw-blonde letting fly a fist at beauty's mid-section.

THE slamming marathon was a hot success. On the night of the ball, Ina slid into those little gentleman-size shorts like a foot into a sock. The pink velvet pants actually flapped, and Ina hurried forth to the fray in a mood to march through Georgia and points south. Jack Gilbert never had a chance. Not that he wanted to make a second guess. He took one look at this pink human eel gliding around under the seductive lights of the hotel patio and let his feet skate out from under him.

Sylvia's guess is that the famous elopement of the pair to Las Vegas two weeks later was figured out that night.

For, the very next day, Ina began to worry about a matter she had tucked away in the back of her mind during the excitement. She had come to Hollywood engaged to her eastern beau, Gene Markey, the writer. And Gene was due any day with flowers and a ring.

It was funny to watch poor Ina try to dope out what to do about that one. In the end she did what most women do in a similar situation—nothing.

At the last minute, with the plane chartered in which Jack was going to fly his bride and the witnesses to Las Vegas for the ceremony-on-the-wing, Ina got an attack of little-girl-itis. Maybe she thought she was in a tough spot, with no mother to guide her—or something. Anyway, she confided to Sylvia that she had wanted to take her along as her witness. "I had a sort of feeling there was nobody

98

on my side," was the way she put it. "And, anyway, in a way you're responsible, Sylvia. You made me into what Jack likes."

If Sylvia wasn't in on the elopement flight she was in on what followed. It was this way. The flight to Nevada was so timed as to bring the newlyweds back to Jack's house by dusk. Five minutes after Ina was inducted into her new home, Sylvia's phone was ringing. Sylvia being out on her rounds, I answered. Ina was on the wire, all fussed and upset. Sylvia must come over right away—right away! Did I understand? I did, but had to answer that the boss was out on her rounds and wouldn't be where the message could reach her until late in the evening.

"Oh, dear!" came a sigh from Ina. "And I've never needed her so badly as right now! Well, tell her to get over here the first thing in the morning, without fail!"

So it came about that Sylvia awakened the new bride. Reporting at Jack Gilbert's house early next

99

morning, she was promptly ushered into a charming bedroom where she found Ina alone.

"Have you the papers?" was Ina's first excited, high-pitched question. "What are they saying about me?"

Sylvia shrugged. She hadn't thought to bring the morning papers. Ina fretted, but a maid brought in a pile of papers just then and she dived into them.

Breakfast was brought in and the bride was still Oh-ing and Ah-ing over the headlines and the telegraph items from Chicago telling about how Gene Markey, on his way West to take a wife, had stopped off in his home town and taken a temperature instead.

Jack, all spruced up and swathed in a silk gown, came in from his dressing-room and added to the excitement. The newly-weds tore the papers from each other's hands. Someone thought to set a third place at table for Sylvia, and soon all three were hard at it combing the press for further items,

100

while the coffee—and who knows? maybe love too —were getting cold.

For an odd incident made a sudden coolness over that frantic breakfast table.

Sylvia, gleaning, noticed a report of the elope- ment that had not been read. Over the report was the heading: INA CLAIRE MARRIES JACK GILBERT. Sylvia passed the sheet to Ina, reading the headline aloud, and Ina grabbed—but not as quickly as did Jack.

The bridegroom cried, "What?" and tore the sheet from Sylvia's hands. "Isn't that silly?" he exclaimed. "They got that headline wrong."

"How, darling?" inquired the bride.

"Why, for news value," declared Jack, "they should have turned it around: JACK GILBERT MARRIES INA CLAIRE."

He carried it off with a laugh. But Ina didn't laugh. And Sylvia had to rush in and fill a con- versational pause.

A funny angle on the Gilbert-Claire marriage, which Sylvia heard about later as she went from one to another of the film folks on her rounds, was that the duration of the romance became a matter of speculation and finally of a gambling pool. The film people, standing on the side lines and watching Ina and Jack struggle, got up a money pool just as they do on shipboard about the ship's daily run. Only, in this case, instead of miles it was time; instead of knots added, it was the reverse—when would a knot slip? Each one who joined the pool bought a certain month. The one who held the slip corresponding to the month in which the marriage went *caput* was to collect.

And now the pool members are much embarrassed. When, exactly, did the romance end? On exactly what day of what month were Ina and Jack unjoined?

For the betters neglected to stipulate that the date of an overt act, such as the filing of a divorce plea, was to settle the issue, and the consensus now is that what was meant was the day on which the principals decided to kick love out of the house.

HER WEDDING NIGHT

INA was making "The Awful Truth" at Pathé when a sudden series of events, involving Gloria Swanson and confronting Sylvia with the necessity for the most momentous decision in her life, ended by establishing the boss as contract masseuse on the Pathé lot. As will appear, Sylvia's Pathé job was to give Gloria Swanson first call on her services, with the other Pathé stars taking whatever time Gloria did not demand.

Well, Ina was one of those who decided not to take Gloria Swanson's leavings. She did not come near Sylvia's workrooms on the Pathé lot.

And then, presently, Gene Markey came out to Hollywood, apparently cured of infatuation for the belle who had given him such a tough break. Gene unconsciously published the fact that he was cured in the way that would annoy Ina worst. He turned up as one of Gloria Swanson's gallants and paid Ina's Pathé-lot rival open and assiduous court.

It's only feminine for a woman to expect a discarded lover to go and picturesquely pine away somewhere. And when Gene perked up so rapidly and began to part his hair and carry flowers to a new shrine, why, Ina got miffed.

Somebody had to be the goat. Sylvia was elected, and has suffered under a decree of banishment which has deprived her of Ina as a patient ever since.

∿∿∿∿∿∿∿∿∿∿∿∿∿∿∿∿∿∿∿∿∿∿∿∿∿∿∿∿

X

THE TOLL OF A BELLE

To give an idea of the semiroyal atmosphere that surrounded Gloria Swanson when the boss went to work on her in the summer of 1929, an adventure that happened to Carmel Myers, an old patient of Sylvia's, is a good illustration.

Carmel once had a rep around Hollywood of being high-hat. Now, being "superior" is the one unforgivable sin in Hollywood. You've got to qualify that, of course. You can high-hat some, and you can't high-hat others. It's very complicated, like irregular verbs in French. On the lot you can high-hat writers, dialogue directors, the man who takes orders for custom-made shirts, people who act in Westerns, and Spaniards. Just now you can also high-hat musicians; but that isn't safe, because nobody knows when musical comedy will come back on us like the seven-year itch. Outside of these few, you can't high-hat anybody. As for all the territory that is *not* a studio lot—even the novice knows that there you can't high-hat a soul. Because everybody outside the profession is Public, and King.

Well, Carmel must have forgotten to say please to a taxi chauffeur once, or something terrible like that, and it got said around that she thought high of herself. The rumor started small, you understand—just a few whispers among the insiders. And Carmel could have stopped it at once. But, as luck would have it, poor Carmel was laid up at the time.

In fact, she had to get out of bed a few days later to answer a summons to the Pathé lot to talk over a rôle with a director. She had the chauffeur drive her down to the old Culver City lot, with its colonial portico, lawn and carriage drive, and

106

guarded gate in the fence. At the gate Carmel's driver came to a stop, and it looked as if Carmel would have to walk the length of the private drive.

At this time Gloria Swanson was making her United Artists pictures on the Pathé lot, as what you might call a paying-guest artist. In other words, Joe Kennedy, her production manager, paid the Pathé people for the privilege of using the Pathé stages. So Gloria was in the position of star boarder in the old colonial homestead—and never was star boarder treated better than was Gloria by everybody, from highest executive to humblest doorman, on the Pathé lot.

As has been mentioned, the entrance to the lot is a curved driveway leading up to the executive offices in a building of colonial design. There was a tacit understanding, which the old gateman administered like a commandment carved in stone, that Gloria was the only hired hand whose car had the privilege of passing the grilled gates and depositing its passenger in the pillared portico.

On the day and the minute of Carmel Myers'

arrival before the Pathé doors, Gloria's car happened to shoot out of a side street and dash through the quickly opened gates. Carmel, who was about to get out of her car and start up the driveway on foot, saw the gates swing open and, breathing a sigh of relief, sank back in her seat and ordered her chauffeur to follow the other car in.

The old gateman almost fainted when the strange car dashed past and up the drive. He gesticulated and howled. But by this time Carmel was out of her car and across the porch into the Pathé building. Poor Carmel never knew, until some time afterward, that she had been guilty of a crime of desecration. Who did she think she was— Will Hays or somebody? That was what the scandalized people on the Pathé lot said.

A few weeks later, Carmel was lying on the slab in our back room resting up from a treatment. It's the moment for confidences in a massage parlor. Lying there with all the bones loosened up, the patient's jaw gets likewise and begins to chew over the secret troubles.

"Sylvia," says Carmel all of a sudden, "have you ever heard them say I'm high-hat?"

Well, the boss had to admit that that was just what she had been hearing. In fact, the patient before Carmel had been telling Sylvia all about the Pathé-lot incident, and how Carmel had dared to use the motor driveway for motor driving.

"So you heard about that, did you?" said Carmel, and told her tale of woe.

"It just goes to show how you can get judged unfairly," she started, and told how she had followed Swanson's car up the driveway without giving a thought to whether it was correct or not. "In fact"—she took that back—"I *did* wonder whether I ought to or not, but look!"

And Carmel peeled off her stocking and showed Sylvia a sore foot.

"It's an ingrown toenail!" wailed Carmel. "And two days before I went over to Pathé, the pedicure cut it open. I was going around with one shoe, and it hurt like toothache every time I put my bum foot down. Before they opened those gates

109

for Gloria's car, I was sitting there in my car just crying—thinking about walking up that nasty long drive. And when those gates opened I didn't hesitate: I just told the driver to shoot on in."

And that is the true story of how Carmel Myers, because of a sore big toe, got known as a case of big sore head.

For the sake of the point, I've got a little ahead of the order of events, which should begin with one fateful week-end in the earliest days of the talkies, during which Sylvia was offered and took the contract to do her thumping and mangling exclusively for Pathé.

THE general hysteria among the movie stars that accompanied the advent of sound in the movie industry had a lot to do with the sudden change in Sylvia's fortunes. Those were the days when the fate of every star was in the balance. And the dear girls knew it. The Marne for everybody, and how they all fought! The favored tactics were to hunt for allies—vocal teachers, elocutionists, voice

110

placers, and what not. Names since forgotten leaped into prominence—Italian names mostly, of teachers of *bel canto*.

In the midst of all this nonsense one star kept her head—Norma Talmadge. While the rest were all signing up Italians and Frenchmen and Spaniards to teach them how to speak the English tongue, Norma quietly sneaked off to New York and came back to Hollywood with Laura Hope Crews, cultured and expert product of the Broadway stage. And instantly everybody knew that Norma had bagged big game while the rest of the sorority had been busy bringing down sparrows. Miss Crews came out to coach Norma in her first talkie.

Meanwhile, Gloria Swanson had been holding off. Smart enough to see that the others were throwing away their good money on quacks and fakes, but still bewildered by it all, Gloria simply did nothing. Incidentally, though, she worried enough to etch a few lines in her face and increase her girth by a few inches. (Worry, says Sylvia, is the prime cause of overweight in most cases.)

The date for starting work on Gloria's first talkie, Edmund Goulding's "The Trespasser," was fast approaching, and Gloria had still done nothing about correcting the lisp that was characteristic of all old-line movie stars in their first essays before the microphone—and also nothing about getting into physical condition.

It's like Gloria to put off decisions until the last minute, and then make them suddenly—and right!

She went to Norma Talmadge to ask for the "loan" of Laura Hope Crews. And she moved to get a corner on the boss's services as a masseuse. With Norma Talmadge, Gloria was open and honest. She went with Edmund Goulding, who knew Miss Crews, and the two of them put up to her and Norma Talmadge a request that the former might supervise the dialogue of "The Trespasser." Miss Crews took a shine to Gloria, Norma Talmadge gave her blessing, and the Crews-Swanson association was launched.

Gloria played fair with Norma Talmadge. In

112

the course of developments, others did not similarly play fair with Gloria.

Then, instead of an elocution lesson, the first thing Laura Hope Crews gave Gloria was advice to get in physical trim, and to that end to hire Sylvia. The call for the boss came on a Saturday night and, as usual, was given like a three-alarm. It was Gloria's secretary on the phone—and Sylvia simply *must* come over right away (the hour being 10 P.M.).

Well, you don't turn down Gloria Swanson. The boss beat it over to Gloria's famous house on Sunset Boulevard.

∿∿

XI

FAT CHANCE

GLORIA runs quite an establishment—butlers, footmen, and the rest. Down on the Pathé lot she rolled up her sleeves and did her day labor like an old trouper. But at home she was La Marquise de la Falaise et de la Coudraye, and had the big soft rugs, uniformed servants, and all the dog to prove it.

The house staff gave Sylvia the works, which is to say that she passed through about ten pairs of hands, to land finally in an upstairs den. There time passed in great chunks without any sign of Gloria Swanson. The boss was dead tired and had to pinch herself to keep awake. Whereupon a footman am-

bled in with a clinking tray, and she tried just one
for luck and was sunk.

She had no idea what time it was when, presently, someone shook her out of a sound sleep and
said: "Here I am—all ready for you."

It was Gloria in her nightie. A clear case of
overwrought nerves, with the inevitable results of
facial lines and general puffiness. The treatment for
that is delicate. If you start in pounding and pum-
meling at the start, the subject's nerves get worse
and worse, and the result you're likely to get is the
kind of weight reduction that is ruin—a stringy,
jumpy body and a cavernous, drawn look about the
face.

In the first few minutes Gloria admitted that
the new sound-movie racket had her half-crazy. It
took the boss two hours of gentle, soothing rubbing
to get the overexcited star to sleep. Meanwhile she
was told that the job would take time; that, for a
start, she'd have to reconcile herself to getting
maybe a little fatter than she was; that the real

115

work on her hips, chin, and arms would have to wait. Gloria saw the point and said:

"Then I'll have to have you all the time. You've got to give up your other people and work for me alone."

Right away the boss remembered how that hook-up had worked out with Mae Murray—and even with Mary Duncan. It meant having to build up her clientele all over again when the contract died.

THE offer from Gloria was flattering enough. But the boss had got past the point where the name of a movie star, whispered, was enough to jerk her out of a sound sleep. She was able to keep her head when Swanson made her offer, because, for one thing, the savings account was doing nicely, and, for another, she had just taken on Norma Shearer, whom she had been angling to get for months.

Hedda Hopper steered Norma Shearer into Sylvia's hands. At that, the boss nearly lost the M.-G.-M. star after the first treatment, which was given in Shearer's home. Norma had been playing a lot of tennis, and had got stringy and muscular and jumpy, the way women always do when they go crazy about any sport. The first thing to do was to calm her down and get her to sleeping regularly as a preliminary to softening her. So the boss rubbed her for nearly two hours and left her sleeping like a child. The next morning we got a phone call from Hedda Hopper, who said:

"I don't know what you did to Norma Shearer, Sylvia, but my name is mud in the movies if you've ruined her."

"Why, what's the matter?" asked Sylvia.

"She's half crazy," wept Hedda. "I'm with her now. She's in the next room and Irving's with her" (Irving being Norma's husband and the big guy on the M.-G.-M. lot) "and they're sorry I ever brought you to her."

"But tell me what's wrong!" cried Slyvia.

"That's what *I'd* like to know," said Hedda. "Norma has funny marks—sort of red ruffles—in

117

her skin, all down one side and on her arm and leg on that side."

Well, with a few more hysterical words Hedda conveyed the idea that Mr. Thalberg and Norma and Hedda herself were convinced that Sylvia had crossed up a nerve or something and that Norma was getting paralysis. Because they had read somewhere that paralysis attacks one side of the body, and all these marks were on the same side.

The boss got frightened herself and hopped over to the Thalberg house in her pyjamas. She found them hanging over Norma in bed. Norma was keeping her nerve—suspecting the worst, but heroic withal—and was consoling Irving with the idea that maybe it was all for the best; that she had had all the principal thrills of a movie career anyway, and maybe now it was the hand of Providence pointing out that she should give it up and be a wife and mother. It was an affecting and tragic scene.

They didn't shriek at Sylvia, but Hedda, with a simple dramatic gesture full of noble dignity, merely led the boss to the sufferer's bedside and pulled back the sheet. Sylvia took one look and let out a laugh. Then she slid her hand under the incipient paralytic's body and yanked out a coarse linen ribbed bath towel. Norma had slept all night on the towel which had been used the evening before as a massage mat, and naturally the side which had pressed on the ribbed towel all those hours was marked like a waffle. She has a delicate skin, anyway, that takes a mark like chamois kid.

In spite of being relieved of her fear, Norma wasn't sure she would continue Sylvia's treatments, and needed to be nursed and patted back into client humor. If the boss took Gloria Swanson's offer and told Shearer that she would have to wait three months for her next massage, it was certain to mean a famous customer offended and lost.

Besides Norma Shearer, the boss, right then, was regularly handling Mary Duncan, Alice White, Carmelita Geraghty, Hedda Hopper, Laura Hope Crews, Ina Claire, Norma Talmadge, Elsie Janis, Ramon Novarro, Ruth Chatterton, Ronald

Colman, Ernest Torrence, Jack Holt, Douglas Mac-Lean, Sue Carol, Nick Stuart, Douglas Fairbanks, Jr., Charles Farrell, Virginia Valli, Zasu Pitts, Marion Davies, and a bunch of others. A fat chance they'd all stay put and wait for Sylvia three months while she handled one star exclusively.

The boss put all this up to Gloria. Gloria didn't say anything—just nodded. And a few minutes later she mysteriously asked: "Will you be at home tomorrow?"

Looking at the clock, which showed 3 A. M., Sylvia opined she'd spend what was left of tomorrow in bed.

The next day, a Sunday, the boss was dragged out of bed to talk to a man on the phone who would give his name only to her. He said: "This is Joe Kennedy—Miss Swanson's producer. What would you think of a contract with Pathé? Figure out what you make and we'll beat the figure."

Fair enough. If they beat Sylvia's figure, she'd beat Swanson's.

And, moreover, this wasn't burying herself.

120

The proposition was for the boss to hang out her shingle on the Pathé lot. Primarily, she was to treat Gloria at any and all hours of the day, within reason. Secondarily, she was to give additional time to other Pathé employees, as designated by the management. Then, if there was any time left over, she could give it to a chosen number of her old clients not Pathé employees. For this, $750 weekly. Not bad—not bad!

BEFORE Kennedy went through with signing the contract Monday morning, he wanted to test out Sylvia. A hard-headed business man, Kennedy. What if this was all a lot of hokum? What if Pathé was going to spend a lot of its good money on a faker with a good line? Kennedy proposed to test out Sylvia in person. Would she report at once to his office and give him a treatment?

"For what?" promptly asked Sylvia.

"That's for you to find out," came back Kennedy. If Sylvia was so good, she was supposed to spot what his trouble was.

121

That was the proposition. The boss accepted. She wondered what kind of an old fatty with a watch chain and sideburns she was going to encounter. Her idea of a production manager was something like a cartoon banker.

The man who received her gave her a shock. Kennedy turned out to size up as a youngish Irishman with an athletic build—though that might be his tailor. The boss said so. She added: "Let's see what's under the tailoring. Take your clothes off."

Kennedy got fussed. A deadlock. But the boss wasn't going to give a treatment through five thicknesses of tweed and underwear. It got to be a dare, and he stripped—stripped down to something in which it was going to be hard to find the trouble he had talked about. It turned out he had been a football star and was used to keeping in pretty good athletic condition. Outside of a little excess weight, there was nothing to pick on. Suddenly the boss had a hunch and told Kennedy to walk around the room. The minute he moved, she spotted the trouble—flat feet, the universal complaint of athletes. She named it.

"You win," acknowledged Kennedy. There was no more argument about the contract, except a weak one put up later by the Pathé money man, Bill Sistrom. He tried to argue that she ought to take a smaller salary.

"Let's argue about whether it's seven hundred and fifty or a thousand," suggested the boss—and Sistrom almost put out her eye with the fountain pen.

In the first week at Pathé a comical situation arose, due to nothing but the terrific vanity, ten times as intense as was ever any woman's, of the male. Sylvia was signed to handle Gloria and the second-string Pathé beauties—meaning female beauties, not handsome executives.

Well, believe it or not, the swell lookers in pants in the executive department interpreted the clause about "and others" in the contract to apply to themselves and began taking up the new beauty specialist's time to such an extent that Helen

123

Twelvetrees, Carole Lombard, Ilka Chase, and some of the other Pathé girls often lost out, or had to wait until late in the evening. There were even times when Gloria herself sat around twiddling her thumbs while Sylvia was bringing out the perfect oval of some supervisor's mug.

And—was it health these gentlemen wanted? Not so's you could notice it. What they wanted was beauty—melting, luscious beauty.

The boss claims she's never handled a man yet who didn't hem and haw and eventually get around to hinting that what he really needed was a good facial. The boys have an invariable artifice for getting around to it.

"What a day!" they begin, meaning that the tremendous executive responsibilities have worn them down to wrecks. Then they glance in a mirror. "It shows on a fellow, doesn't it?"

Sylvia just waits, knowing what's coming next. Some of them are brisk and offhand; some stammer; but they all say about the same thing: "If you just went over my face and neck, mama,

124

I think it would get my nerves in shape for the day's work."

Five minutes later, if Sylvia gives them the facial they've been plotting to get, they're talking about blackheads and wrinkles and their chin line like any woman turning forty and scared of losing her profile.

Before Sylvia had been on the Pathé lot a month, handling Gloria and whacking and paddling her through "The Trespasser" shooting, she was up against something much tougher to handle than the smirking vanities of the front-office executives. It was the resentment kindled in the breasts of the other feminine stars on the lot by the fact that they all had to defer to Gloria in the matter of securing treatment appointments.

Ina Claire revolted openly—steered clear of the bungalow assigned to Sylvia for her labors— and got her own private pummeler.

Others grumbled. Nobody, however, challenged Gloria's right to first call until, one day, following a string of advance reports, a new comet

125

landed with a whiz on the old Culver City lot and promptly gave out sparks and fizzes promising trouble.

But the story of Constance Bennett belongs to a new chapter.

∿∿∿∿∿∿∿∿∿∿∿∿∿∿∿∿∿∿∿∿∿∿∿∿∿∿∿∿∿∿∿∿∿∿∿∿∿∿∿

XII

THE TORTURE CHAMBER

THE boss's bungalow on the Pathé lot got to be a hangout. Rumors got around about what went on in there. The little stucco shack got christened the Torture Chamber.

Ann Harding and her husband, Harry Bannister, were a bit responsible for the reputation of the inner chamber where the boss did her pounding. At the time, Ann was pretty unfit, meaning somewhat overweight, and she was pretty vocal about letting the world know it when Sylvia was pinching pleats out of her.

Moreover, Ann refused to see that a movie career and all the money were worth the bother

127

and would intimate that, any time she got fed up, she would leave the movies flat and go back East.

So the Pathé executives would sneak over and implore Sylvia to do two things: take flesh off Ann *but* not hurt her. Which two things don't go together. So Sylvia would compromise by taking the flesh off Ann *and* hurting her, same as with anyone else. Bannister would hang around outside the shack while Ann was getting her treatment, smoking cigarettes nervously, like a man waiting to hear if it's a boy, and when Ann let out a yell, he would bust in with his hair bristling and his jaw set and stop the horrible proceedings.

As a matter of fact, a vigorous massage, when the client's trouble is fat, does hurt a bit. But the reason for the howls that arose in Sylvia's operating room was more the pampered sensitiveness of the patients than any agony connected with the method.

The real reason for the phenomenal success of massage in the film colony is that it's a short-cut to physical conditioning, without which beauty

128

turns into so much lard, and it's a method where the responsibility is shifted to other shoulders. The victims on Sylvia's slab in the back room of the Pathé bungalow took punishment—plenty! But not without howls and shrieks of agony that drew the attention of the executive department. On a hot, quiet day the outcries from the bungalow would reach the street outside the lot.

It wasn't the public scandal the Pathé executives minded. What worried them was the possible effect on morale on the lot. It was getting so that the frightened actors made up all sorts of excuses to get out of taking their turns on the slab. So the Pathé people went into conference and decided to put a radio set with an oversize loud-speaker in Sylvia's bungalow. The plug for switching on the music was put handy to the slab. When Sylvia was ready to go to work on a pair of bulging hips or an inflated tummy, she just gave the radio switch a slip and the loud-speaker started a squawk that drowned out the cries of the victim.

A GOOD deal of the work on the lot consisted in setting up folks who had had a tough night—or who were simply "sunk" from nerves and lack of sleep. So one of the important pieces of equipment was an electric percolator. The best pick-me-up in the world, for quick results, is a cup of ink-black coffee, without sugar, but with about a teaspoonful of lemon juice in it.

Having hot coffee on tap, it was simple to lay in a few supplies, and the joint got to be a quick-lunch. Service started about 7:30 A.M., and there was usually a mob. You see, between the front-office men and Gloria Swanson, the boss was booked for later hours, and those who didn't have the drag that Gloria had soon learned to get in their treatments bright and early.

Dorothy Mackaill was one of the regulars. At that time Dot was a holdout over at the First Na-'
tional lot. The situation was telling on her. She was losing a lot of sleep. Each morning she would arrive earlier.

Another regular was Peppy Lederer, Marion

130

Davies' niece. Peppy was trying hard to break into the movies, and Marion sent her over to be beautified.

Alan Hale was the male element. He was doing a picture in which he was a sailor. The costume department handed him a pair of sailor pants that had been worn by Billy Boyd in a successful picture, and Alan got a hunch that the pants were lucky.

Alan Hale set much store by Billy Boyd's sailor pants, but it so happened that Bill was narrower in the beam than Alan. Rather than let out a seam, Alan decided to fit himself to the pants, and put it up to Sylvia to do the whittling. One morning he was on the slab when a hurry-call came from Gloria Swanson's bungalow. Sylvia had to quit half through his treatment, and just when, having finished off the starboard side, she was set to make the larboard symmetrical. To this day he claims that his two halves don't match.

To show there were no hard feelings, Alan left an inscribed photograph on the slab where Sylvia

131

abandoned him. The inscription handed her a
laugh: "To Sylvia—She lives off the fat of the
'hams.' ALAN HALE."

TAKING it by and large, the fat with the lean, the
work on the Pathé lot was turning out pleasant
enough. The pets quarreled among themselves,
naturally, but not obstreperously. The fat rolled
off and the money rolled in—and everything was
jake.

And then Connie Bennett turned up.

Pathé scouts had trailed the newest recruit to
Paris and, over there, had got her to sign on the
dotted line. After which they sent a bushel of raves
by cable, saw La Bennett off on the boat, and sent
a final blast of cables to the general effect: "Oh,
boy! Wait till you see her!"

For the next few weeks executives on the lot
sat around gnawing their knuckles and calling up
railroad information to ask if it looked as if next
month's trains would be on time.

What I'm trying to convey is that Connie

132

THE TORTURE CHAMBER

Bennett's arrival in Hollywood was built up like a musical-comedy entrance: Ta-da, ta-da—here comes the queen!

And, after Bennett got here, she personally saw to it that the excitement didn't die down for want of fuel.

But the first effect she made on the Pathé people was—well, let's tell what happened.

Sylvia got her first impression of the newcomer at second hand. She didn't lay eyes on her for a while, but she looked at the faces of Joe Kennedy and Bill Sistrom every morning, and she saw, by the way they began developing complexion troubles, that something was wrong. The boys didn't say anything, exactly; but when they were asked when Bennett was going to start her first picture, they stalled and turned sort of green.

Finally Joe Kennedy dropped into Sylvia's shack for the unusual purpose of inviting the boss to dinner.

Well, Joe Kennedy saw enough of the boss daytimes to be able to stand an evening away from her, and Sylvia, figuring there was a catch in it somewhere, asked him:

"And what do I do for the eats?"

"Well," said Mr. Kennedy, trying to be casual, and failing, "Miss Bennett'll be there."

The boss understood. She was to be present to do her magic undressing act, which, as you shall see, is accomplished without removing a pin or a button.

Maybe this is a point that doesn't need explaining, but it might be mentioned that Hollywood buys its beauty pretty blind. They say that on Broadway they don't hire their stage lookers without having pretty well satisfied themselves, by personal inspection, that it's all true—not wooden legs and stuffing. But the Hollywood boys, devilish fellows though they may be, buy their stars pretty much the way the average citizen shops for a wife —nothing to go on but having once helped the wench into a taxi. And their chances aren't much better than the average citizen's in the same spot. Men are such boobs at judging a woman's points!

134

THE TORTURE CHAMBER

But even Joe Kennedy could see that there was something the matter with Bennett. The question that was turning his hair gray was, what? He wanted Sylvia's expert opinion.

So here was the Kennedy dinner party collected—all but Sylvia, late as usual. Gloria Swanson, Laura Hope Crews, and Constance Bennett were the ladies; Kennedy and a couple of other tuxedos made up the company. After a while the boss breezed in. She took one look at the fair guest from over the seas and got medical.

"You look rotten, baby," she started in. "What've you been doing to yourself? Not sleeping?"

Joe Kennedy had failed to tip off the newcomer about Sylvia's habits and customs, and Bennett took the outburst like a sock on the chin. The others were trying to give Sylvia the high-sign to go easy, but it's hard to stop the boss once she's started. And, anyway, her understanding was that she was supposed to do her usual act.

"The girl's sick," Sylvia lectured the other

135

guests, something like a doctor demonstrating to medical students. "Look. No flesh on her face. And"—she turned Bennett around—"and you could play a xylophone solo on your backbone, baby."

Bennett began to look miserable. "I *have* been sick," she protested. "I lost pounds and pounds in Paris. This isn't the way I look, at all."

"Of course not," confirmed Sylvia.

And then Kennedy managed to change the subject and, presently, to get Sylvia off into the hall, where he gave her hell for tearing into his guest that way, but ended up by anxiously inquiring: "Is that right—what she said about it's all being due to sickness?"

"Sure; she's a swell looker when she's fit," opined Sylvia.

What worried the technical people and cameramen more than anything else was that back, on which the vertebræ could be counted. The actress was scheduled for a series of those high-society comedies where about half the scenes are views

136

of the heroine's bare back. And no magic of lighting would disguise the fact that every joint in this
spine threw a shadow.

When the boss went to work to cover the bones
called Bennett with some photographable flesh,
production of Connie's first talkie, "Rich People,"
was postponed, waiting on the star's rounding into
shape. She looked more like poor people than rich
people when Sylvia started massaging.

Connie was plainly a product of the metropo-
lises, one of those high-bred, high-strung girls. As
restless and jumpy as a flea, the new star seemed
to have a horror of being alone. Sylvia was treating her at her home. The preliminary work was a
nightly rubbing of a gentle kind, to induce sleep,
and it had to be done in the bed the patient was
to occupy for the night.

Right away the boss had a job that isn't usually considered part of a masseuse's vocation.
Every night she had to clear Bennett's apartment
of an assortment of friends and companions who
couldn't get it through their silly heads that an

137

order given by a hired rubber that their hostess was to be in bed at nine each night was meant to be obeyed. The first few evenings, when Sylvia turned up and yanked Bennett off to bed at the stipulated hour, the merry company was all for crowding into the bedroom with the card table and the glasses and helping out the health program with cigarette smoke and close harmony.

The effect of going back to a babyhood régime—sleep with the sun and fattening messes for meals—soon developed Bennett into the hot looker she really is. "Rich People" got under way, and you could hear the Pathé executives whistling at their work through the open windows in the main offices.

Everything was lovely.

∿∿∿∿∿∿∿∿∿∿∿∿∿∿∿∿∿∿∿∿∿∿∿∿

XIII

BATTLE ROYAL

AND then, one day, Bennett had to wait because Sylvia was busy on Swanson. That was the match that touched off the fireworks.

They were waiting to be touched off, according to the rumors of a private difference between the two. Anyway, it was plain on the lot, from the first, that Connie and Gloria weren't going to get along. It's dangerous putting two such high-powered belles in the same county, let alone on the same movie lot, where all everybody ever does in idle hours is try to steal one another's water coolers, jobs, mascara, and boy friends.

139

One thing you've got to say for Bennett: she doesn't avoid a fight when she sees it coming. On the contrary, she sticks to the good old principle— applied equally by school kids, prize fighters, Napoleon, and professional belles—that the first sock is likely to win.

From week to week Bennett was getting more and more restless about the one thing on the Pathé lot that no one had ever yet dared to contest—the admitted fact that the sun was a big Klieg light created for the purpose of making a camera halo around Gloria Swanson's hair, and that any of its light that happened to fall on anyone else was graciously permitted to do so by Swanson Productions, Inc.

It's about time to take a side glance at one of the elements of this general situation which has been neglected—the snatching and grabbing of boy friends that went on under the surface. If you go back to the moment when all these ladies were in different parts of the earth, satisfied with their re-

140

spective lots and loves, you find that, in the way of pairings, all were contented.

Ina Claire had her Gene Markey. Gloria Swanson had her Marquis Henri. Greta Garbo had her Jack Gilbert. Connie Bennett had her health.

Ina started the war when she busted up the combination by grabbing off Jack Gilbert. That left Gene Markey a lone wolf, and the long moon-shiny nights in the Beverly foothills were filled with baleful bachelor bayings.

ANOTHER thing Ina did when she swooped out of the East and rustled herself a branded bull out of the contented herd was to set up a sort of self-conscious stir among the other females. Example is contagious.

And the wisest ones saw at a glance what was the trouble, the chronic Hollywood trouble, cause of most of the ructions that set the news wires periodically to humming.

Out here there aren't enough Class A-1 boy friends to go around. What I mean is blue-ribbon

141

boy friends with stars in their foreheads, the kind that throw sod over into the next pasture when they start snorting and pawing the ground.

At the time of Connie Bennett's arrival there were only two real pedigreed prancing papas on the prairie—Jack Gilbert and the Marquis Henri de la Falaise. Others? Oh, sure, there are others. But I don't mean others. I mean sirloin. I mean the kind that can flip a hoof and shoot sand right over the Rockies into the Eastern public eye.

Right now it looks as if the town at last has got one more boy friend to fight over. Gene Markey has been coming right along ever since his arrival here, just after he hit front pages as Ina Claire's discardboard lover. Maybe that wasn't such a good start; but a front page is a front page, whether you hit it in a graceful pose or on your ear. Right away Gene made himself felt, so to speak.

Anyhow, when Gloria Swanson found herself without an escort, it was a civic scandal. Gene saw what was wrong and, public-spirited citizen that he is, walked up and set it right. The neighbors went back to watering their lawns, and the consensus was that Markey had been sent by heaven to fill an aching void.

There was a momentary calm—only a breathing spell between rounds of the battle royal, as will be seen; but for a while everybody settled down in a neutral corner and caught a deep breath.

In fact, deceived by appearances, Gloria Swanson took a chance and went away. She finished "The Trespasser," saw the film released, assured herself that it was a hit, and breezed for Paris and a little vacation from the toil and heartache of Hollywood.

On the way East, she stopped off in Chicago and gave Sylvia the biggest break she ever had. The Chicago reporters interviewed Gloria and told her she was looking like a million dollars, and Gloria shoved the boss into the news by telling the boys that her face and form had been tailored for "The Trespasser" rôle by a masseuse out in Hollywood who asked you what you wanted to be—

143

Venus or Diana—and then slapped you into a ringer for either one, take your choice.

OUT in Hollywood, things were quiet on the Pathé lot. Swanson was headed for Paris. Joe Kennedy had gone to New York. With the big boss away, all the little people were happy. And with Swanson absent, Bennett ranked supreme and was happy too. But Bennett was smart enough to know that she would have to step down into second place again when Gloria came home. Unless——

Well, Bennett apparently decided that the best time to attack the enemy's positions is when they are undefended.

Sylvia was working on Bennett one day when the Chicago interview given by Gloria was printed in a local paper. Bennett had been reading the blurb. She looked up from the page and asked Sylvia: "Do you think it's true that you got Swanson in shape for 'The Trespasser'?"

"Figure it out for yourself," said the boss, always the shrinking violet. "Do you remember what *you* looked like before I took hold of you?"

Bennett didn't say anything, just looked as if there was a bit of strategy on her mind. She kept her thoughts to herself until the rubdown was well under way, and then she came back to what was bothering her. She took a new angle.

"Working on Gloria was a great break for you, wasn't it?" she said to Sylvia. "It's making you famous."

She was lying face down, but she twisted around to look at Sylvia as she continued.

"If you want to be famous all over the world, I could set you in places where Swanson wouldn't even get invited. Look here"—and she turned completely around and sat up. "Do you want to massage the King of Spain?"

Sylvia didn't have the answer for that and let Bennett rave on.

"I could take you first to Paris and fix you up there so that every celebrity in the world would patronize you. Not just movie actors, either—but real people. And then I'd take you down to Spain.

145

I know everybody in Spain. You know—people of the royal court. What do you say?"

Sylvia said it with a whack that laid the temptress out on the slab in position for finishing the treatment.

In the next few days Bennett returned incessantly to the subject. What she proposed was that Sylvia accompany her abroad, leaving the Pathé people to like it or take whatever other course they saw fit. Plainly, only one interpretation was to be put on Bennett's move. She had it firmly in her head that Sylvia was the secret of Swanson's beauty. The brains of these professional beauties act like that.

It's their private thoughts that give them those dimples we all adore.

THE amazing development that came next was that, way off in Paris, Gloria got wind of what was going on. Call it female telepathy, or assume that some dear friend of both girls spent five dollars on a week-end cablegram just as an investment in fun

—the fact was that Joe Kennedy, sitting in the Pathé offices in New York with nothing but booking and release dates on his mind, was suddenly jerked out of his seat by a radiogram from Gloria, who had set sail for home.

The message was full of anger and hurt, and informed Kennedy that Connie Bennett, the so-and-so, was kidnaping Gloria's Sylvia from the home lot, and would Joe please call out the militia and start action at once against Bennett for mayhem and points south.

Sylvia was over in Bennett's suite late that night, giving the lady her go-to-sleep patting, when the phone bell rang. Sylvia heard one side of the ensuing conversation, but pricked up her ears when she realized that the call was from New York and that herself was the subject thereof.

"I only asked her to accompany me on my trip to Europe," Bennett was telling Kennedy at the other end of the wire. Judging by Bennett's frequent pauses and the way she winced and explained, she was getting a bawling out.

147

"I don't see why Swanson misjudges me that way," she complained into the phone. "Why, I— I——"

Again she was silenced by an outburst from Kennedy, who raised his voice so high that his words could be heard by Sylvia.

"Is that double-crossing little bum Sylvia with you now?" he yelled.

Connie Bennett started to deny, but Sylvia was at her elbow, grabbing for the phone. She passed it over and Sylvia called into the mouth-piece: "Here I am."

Then she blinked and spluttered and tried to cut in for about two minutes while Joe Kennedy called her names. According to Joe's information, Sylvia was a traitor and a renegade and a few other things. And Bennett was—oh, well, a movie actress. And the two of you, boil your hides, are conspiring to do Gloria dirt. And after all Gloria has done for the boss! Joe Kennedy almost cried.

Which anyway gave Sylvia a chance to say the first word she had got in.

148

"But I'm not accepting Miss Bennett's offer!" she shrieked. "And you can go to——!" And she hung up.

She turned around to go for Bennett as cause of all her woe, maybe cause of her losing out with Pathé and being put out of a swell job. But all that Bennett listened to was the part about Sylvia's Pathé connection being in danger. She pounced on that.

"Certainly," she agreed. "Now the Pathé people will look for a chance to kick you out. Don't wait for that to happen. Come to Europe with me."

She was feverishly excited about putting it over. You'd think that she wanted this one thing more than anything else in the world. At the moment, no doubt she did. It was a matter of who wins? Gloria or Connie? And Connie wasn't stopping at anything to make the answer suit her self-esteem.

Sylvia was packing up to get away. She had had enough for one night and she wanted to get home and cry on family shoulders. She turned to say good night to Bennett.

And there was Bennett, sitting up in bed, with her hand stretched out so that it was under the spotlight from the bed-table lamp. She had a star-sapphire ring on one finger that Sylvia had once admired, and she was making the sapphire flash in the light and looking at Sylvia with a coy expression.

Suddenly she stuck her head to one side and pulled the ring off her finger.

"Do you like my ring?" she cooed. "It's yours if you'll come."

And she stretched an arm out over the footboard and tried to put the ring on Sylvia's hand.

Oh, well, the boss got out of there still unpersuaded. She is superstitious. And a few weeks later she was struck all of a heap one day when she happened to notice how "sapphire" is spelled and that you split it up and it just about spells *"Sap Hire."*

Well, the excitement died down, and Sylvia

wasn't fired, and she didn't go over and massage
the King of Spain, and Gloria Swanson came back
to Hollywood and laughed about the whole thing
(the winner's laugh!), and Joe Kennedy came back
and had his treatments as before.

And—and what do you know?—Connie and
Gloria met up after Gloria got back from Paris,
and the two girls kissed and hugged as if one was
a blotter and the other the ink and they loved each
other so much that it was all you could do to—oh,
rats, pass me the bicarbonate!

Mind, I'm not saying there isn't a great kick
in watching a set-to like this between rival screen
beauties. Maybe you'd get the same kick out of being a second to a heavyweight prize fighter of
championship caliber. But the fight for screen supremacy is much subtler than what takes place
around and about the prize ring. For one thing,
the girls aren't supposed to sock. For another,
they're *supposed* to lie back, look their best, and
just wait for the championship to happen to them!

Bennett took the trip to Paris without Sylvia

151

and, somewhere along the road, she adopted a baby. That girl certainly must crave company!

At that, a baby can build up a woman's weight better than a masseuse can. But Connie, the little innocent darling, should be told that it isn't done by *adopting* a baby.

∧∧

XIV

THE PLOT THICKENS—AND SOME MIDRIFFS!

IT SEEMS that the first thing for a high-power beauty to do when she gets into the movies and comes to Hollywood is to go up and give Gloria Swanson a big shove and say: "Yah!"

I don't know why this is, but they all do it. They don't pick on Garbo, or Chatterton, or Shearer. No; they all come into town and go up to the hotel and wash their faces, and beat it out to Sunset Boulevard and Crescent Drive, where Gloria's front lawn comes down to the sidewalk, and get out and walk up and down and sneer

153

and yell: "Come out and fight! I can lick you!"

Why, even Mrs. Patrick Campbell, the London actress who is so veteran that she used to play for one of the Edwards—the VII, I think—even this old-timer had to get a rush of rivalry to her venerable head and take a fall out of Gloria. It was a rather nasty fall, too.

Mrs. Pat saw one of Gloria's films and was all excited about it and went around Hollywood begging to meet "that perfectly chawming gel." And Gloria's friends began to set up the drinks and celebrate, because Mrs. Pat knows Bernard Shaw and that makes her opinion worth its weight in salt. They threw a reception for the woman who has been the toast of London so long, and were tickled to death—until Mrs. Pat, who had been waiting for this spot, added to her honeyed flattery of Gloria the little bit of wormwood which she had been waiting to spill all the while.

"Yes, a dee-*light*ful creature, this Swanson gel; really a pippin, as you Americans say. You

154

THE PLOT THICKENS

know, I've been wondering what it was that struck
me most about that gel and her most striking smile,
and I've just hit on what it is. Really, my dears,
she ought to be told to file down her teeth!"

I GUESS the reason for all the resentment is Gloria's
pull with men. Other movie queens in Hollywood
can give Gloria arguments on picture grosses and
the size of their fan mail, but Gloria's front porch
is the place where all the boys go on the night off.
And Hollywood hostesses have learned not to give
parties in competition with Gloria, because if
they do, the only men they'll get are local movie
critics and assistants in the Hays office.

So the newcomers hear about this and decide
that it's about time to make a change. And they
set out the drinks and the sandwiches, and put on
the low-back gowns, and light up the front parlor
and leave the shades up, and turn on the radio, and
say to themselves: "This'll fetch the boys." And
give a sigh for poor old Gloria and think that she's
going to be pretty lonesome up in that big old

155

house when the sports get wise to the new attraction—but it serves her right for hogging the trade.

But the same thing happens every time. Along about midnight the newcomer puts the sandwiches in the ice box and crawls into bed and lies there wide awake for the next few hours, gnawing her knuckles and listening to the male chorus doing Sweet and Low in twelve verses on Gloria's veranda.

Usually the newcomers calm down after a while and leave Gloria alone, figuring, who wants to take her bunch of amateur tenors away from her, anyway? But every once in a while a born scrapper comes to town who picks herself up after the first knockdown, shakes her head, and squares off to make a finish fight of it. Then Gloria, according to the rules of the game, has to put up her Most Popular Girl championship and accept the challenge.

You saw what happened to Bennett! Well, Grace Moore, having grabbed off honors in musical comedy and grand opera, came to Hollywood

with an M.-G.-M. contract in her bag and a spot of
red in each eye. Bennett and all the other unsuc-
cessful challengers had used the wrong holds on
Gloria. This was going to be different. And the
citizenry were advised to watch Grace's smoke and
make no bets until they'd seen her in a workout.

There was no secret made about Grace's arrival. She rolled into Pasadena in a pair of special
cars so full of secretaries, cats, maids, dogs, and
bandboxes and singing teachers that M.-G.-M. met
the party with busses. The whole outfit concealed
itself modestly in a cottage with twenty-five baths.

Right away there were signs of trouble ahead.
Gene Markey passed up an evening of charades at
Gloria Swanson's manse and went out to the end
of the car line to carry a bouquet to the new singer
from the East. Previous to this incident, Gloria's
crowd had been making some slighting remarks
about the newcomer. They kidded Grace's habit of
appearing everywhere in dense formation—to wit,
surrounded by secretaries and handmaids. Grace
went everywhere like President Hoover riding up

Pennsylvania Avenue; and Swanson partisans
snickered in corners and got up jokes about how
long it took Grace Moore to pass a given point.

But Gene Markey's switch to the rival camp
took the snap out of all the jokes, and Gloria saw
that once again she would have to go out to war.

When Grace's secretary called Sylvia on the
Pathé lot and made a date for his employer to
come down from M.-G.-M. and get treated, Sylvia
hadn't yet been tipped off to the fact that Gloria
and Grace had already exchanged a few snarls.
She thought it was just a new job.

Grace Moore's hour was 5 P.M. the next day.
Vivienne Segal, a veteran of musical comedy who
naturally had her own opinion of Grace Moore
and her "operatic airs," was on the slab from four-
thirty on, and it so happened that Vivienne was
slow about getting into her clothes when five
o'clock came. Which produced a situation, right
off the bat.

It seems that Vivienne had had a manager
who didn't please her, and she had fired him, and

he had come back by filing a suit for damages. And Grace Moore had hired him.

Promptly at five, Sylvia's front office was invaded by a parade. First came a cute-looking chappie in a cutaway and striped pants, a cut-out from the back pages of Vanity Fair, who came as advance scout. He signaled the mob behind him that all was well, and two maids came in and deposited themselves and a lot of Miss Moore's coats on the chairs. Then everybody blew a few trumpets and Grace herself entered slowly and looked around in a pained way, as much as to say:

"What! Am I to be kept waiting?"

The secretary caught the look of annoyance, and spoke up in one of those Eton accents:

"Miss Moore is ready for her treatment."

In the rear room Vivienne Segal suddenly stiffened on the slab and let out a yell:

"Sylvia! Do you hear that voice? That's the man who's suing me!" She jumped to the floor and flung a towel around her. "And you can just tell

159

him for me," she went on, "that if he doesn't get out of here——"

She started for the door to the front room, and Sylvia threw herself into the doorway to cut her off and prevent carnage. There was a sound like a quail rising and, where that secretary had been, stood an empty chair and the hat he left behind.

Grace Moore spoke up.

"Isn't that woman back there taking some of my hour? Please have her leave at once." And Grace waved her hand as if a gesture would dispel a whole flock of Segals.

With that, Vivienne, who had begun to calm down, flew into a new rage.

"*'That woman'!*" she imitated Grace Moore. "Does she mean *me?* Let me go, Sylvia! I'm going to tell her just what I think of her. I'd have her know that Vivienne Segal doesn't dress fast for anybody!"

And she didn't. To show that a woman has her pride, after all, she put both her stockings on

160

wrong side out, and pulled them off and put them on right, all in slow motion, and gave a demonstration of how long a lady can take to powder her nose when she's been riled into a sweat, and finally flounced out triumphantly with her nose in the air.

That was an auspicious beginning, but there's one thing you can count on when you get caught in the center of a Hollywood cat fight: there's always worse to come.

~~~~~~

XV

THE MOORE, THE MERRIER

IN ALL Sylvia's experience, Grace Moore is the only client who has ever managed to undress in a massage parlor without shedding her dignity. The general atmosphere of Sylvia's bungalow being what it was, and the quarters being cramped, our paying guests were usually about as mannerly as dogs in a pound. During business hours the premises usually looked like the banks of the ol' swimmin' hole on a hot Saturday afternoon. People's clothes dropped wherever they stepped out of them, and every so often Sylvia was asked to start a movement whereby everybody

162

traded shirts and stockings until all had their own back again.

But Moore carried her manners with her, as she did everything else except a grand piano—and she would have had the piano brought along if she'd thought of it. The two handmaidens screened Grace into a corner of our two-by-four dressing room and put her through an act like a queen getting ready for bed.

Well, you can put on all the front in the world, but sooner or later you've got to turn around. Five minutes later Sylvia was looking Grace anywhere but in the eye and asking her if opera singers sit a lot between shows.

Grace took it high and mighty at first.

"You must be mistaken," she came back, as loftily as she could. "That sort of thing would show up in a camera test, wouldn't it?"

"You bet it does," assured Sylvia.

"Well, my tests at M.-G.-M. were pronounced perfect," asserted Grace. "And I did one whole scene in profile."

Sylvia didn't argue. But what Grace had said didn't jibe with the confidential call Sylvia had had from the M.-G.-M. lot that morning—an appeal from headquarters to do something about—quarters elsewhere.

Sylvia didn't say anything, but maybe she looked a lot. Anyway, the prima donna went away from the first treatment in a mood of silence that tipped Sylvia off that she might as well expect trouble.

When the trouble came—a "misunderstanding"—the boss made short work of it, and then called up M.-G.-M. to cancel dates for their singing star's further treatments.

And when Grace herself got on the phone a while later, and apologized for the misunderstanding and said everything was lovely, Sylvia froze up like a fjord. Grace's olive branch took the form of an invite to attend a Sunday party up in her hilltop house, and she promised Sylvia some fun.

"I'm going to have M.-G.-M. send over the

trade-mark lion, and Bee Lillie will be there—"
she ballyhooed.

"And I'm supposed to be part of the menagerie?" shouted Sylvia, and hung up the receiver.

But after a while the boss remembered that dough is dough, and the Moore the merrier. Grace came back into the fold. But she continued to act cool and distant. Except, of course, when the boss was beating her a lobster red; everybody is near and hot then.

Grace was getting hot in more places than Sylvia was responsible for. The reason for a steadily mounting temperature in her case was that Gene Markey, whom she had lured away from Gloria Swanson, was showing signs of a relapse.

From its executives down to "MGM," its trade-mark lion, every male on the Metro-Goldwyn-Mayer lot was ready and eager to turn hand-springs to keep Grace in good humor and make her feel that her charm was working on all sixteen. But, being a woman, Grace had to go and look out the window poutingly and long for something she didn't get from Santa Claus! Nothing the M.-G.-M. people could think of could cheer Grace up. On the Metro lot, her director even got Lawrence Tibbett, who was playing opposite Grace in her picture, to give Grace the profile position in all the duet shots. That got a little smile out of the disconsolate belle, but it didn't last long. In a few minutes, down went the corners of her mouth again and she began standing around in corners and moping.

What she really wanted, no doubt, was news that Gloria had broken an ankle—preferably in three places; and though the M.-G.-M. executives can get almost anything they want in Hollywood, they couldn't get that for her.

And then Grace got what she thought a novel idea, not knowing that Mae Murray, Mary Duncan, Connie Bennett, and Ina Claire had all toyed with it before her. In her turn Grace believed the stories that Sylvia was solely responsible for Gloria's hold on beauty. Apparently these girls are all as credulous as belles in the Middle Ages, who used to believe that any looks but their own were got by a pact with Satan, and would fade if you burned a powder made from peacock feathers and said:

"Hocus-pocus, pints and quarts,
  Give her bunions, give her warts."

They thought that if you could take Sylvia away from Gloria for one week, Gloria's looks would deflate.

As Grace began thinking it over, she began to perk up. She planned more astutely than Bennett had, and went about swiping Sylvia in the only way that might work.

Sylvia wasn't even asked; she was just told. And Joe Kennedy did the telling. He had Sylvia up on the carpet in the Pathé front office.

He had just had a telephone call from a Metro-Goldwyn executive, who had said:

"We want to buy up Sylvia's contract, and you may as well sell, because our star, Grace Moore, has practically cinched the matter in private talks with Sylvia, and if you hold Sylvia

167

against her will, what kind of service would you expect to get out of her?"

Later Kennedy pounded the desk and raged. "You're always trying to jump your contract, mama. Gloria Swanson put you where you are. Where's your gratitude?"

Well, when she could get a word in, Sylvia told him that her gratitude was right where it always had been, and told him the facts. When Kennedy got convinced, he began to grin and asked Sylvia:

"Do you suppose Moore talked them into it?"

"Your guess is as good as an affidavit," opined Sylvia, and they agreed to lie back for a few days and see what would happen.

Nothing happened. It looked as if Grace had given it up as a bad job. But Grace has a mustard plaster beaten for stick-to-it-iveness. She was just waiting for a new opening, and the new opening came.

THE MOORE, THE MERRIER

The opening was Gloria Swanson's throat—
and did Grace jump down it?

Gloria was getting ready for her new production, in which she had to sing songs. Well, Gloria's
singing voice isn't her biggest asset, and she was a
little nervous.

In Grace Moore's baggage there was a singing teacher, Signor Marafioti from Italy, who was
supposed to be a regular Svengali who could make
a coloratura out of a trained seal. Gloria heard
about the signor, and the more she tried out her
high C in private, the more convinced she became
that she had to have Marafioti or die.

So this time it was Joe Kennedy calling up
Metro and asking for something *they* controlled.

The Metro executive chuckled in the phone.
"And you're the guy who wouldn't sell us that
masseuse!"

"Have a heart," begged Kennedy. "You don't
know what it is to manage a star with tempera-
ment."

"Oh, don't we!" sort of sighed the Metro man who was managing Grace Moore.

"You and I ought to understand each other," sighed Kennedy in return.

The Metro man said he'd call back that afternoon. In the meantime he had seen Grace Moore. And his proposition, when he phoned, was this:

"You give Grace Moore that rubber, and Grace says she'll give Gloria the signor."

The issue was considered important enough for Pathé to call an executive meeting and discuss the matter, pro and con. They argued all the points and weighed each one, and preferred the masseuse to the music master. They turned Grace Moore and Metro down.

That suits us. Because if anyone high-hats Sylvia now and inquires what standing a masseuse has, she and her art, the boss has her answer ready:

"It's in the records: my racket ranks high— between music and the stars."

170

PART TWO

〰〰〰〰〰〰〰〰〰〰〰〰〰〰〰〰〰〰〰〰〰〰〰〰〰〰〰〰

I

DIET AND WHOLESOME COOKING

1. FOOD AND ITS PREPARATION

BELIEVE it or not, the object of a first-class masseuse's business is to get rid of patients. If she's on the level, the masseuse aims to send the patient away in good condition and hopes never to see her again. In this respect, massage is like the medical profession. The doctors too (the decent ones) do their level best to ruin their own racket and nothing is so satisfactory as a patient cured—which is a patient lost.

In Hollywood, Sylvia is reaching the point where her job, for having been done too well, shows diminishing returns. Which is as it should be. And Sylvia, far from moaning over the fact, is as pleased as the kid who broke up the game by slamming the only ball into the river for a home run. Bit by bit, one by one, the respectable and representative percentage of Hollywood film people who are listed on the boss's books have been made over and educated to the point where they are the caretakers of their own waistlines and do not need professional supervision at thirty dollars an hour.

If the boss can take it that way, far be it from me to show a meaner spirit. So—

Hurrah! I got fired.

It isn't the massage that makes these people their own conditioners. The pounding can, and does, effect a speedy correction of overweight, underweight and some of the other deviations from the beautiful normal. But we can't give any mileage guarantees in our business. A waistline bought on the massaging slab won't last from now until next Sunday unless the buyer coöperates in the upkeep. With every treatment given in our back room goes a lecture on diet. The boss spiels it out while she's working, something like this:

"No more fried food——"

Wham!

"Cut out sea-food."

"Ouch."

"Turn over. And listen: lay off the liquor."

Our customers all go through the same phases. At first they pay no attention to the diet instructions, figuring that the treatments will be absolution for their sins of the table. Sylvia's invariable procedure, after a week or so of this kind of dishonesty, is to lock the patient out. It makes no difference who the patient is. Some of our most famous patients have been through the disciplining experience of being refused treatment. They eat, drink, live and, to a certain extent, dress as Sylvia prescribes, or they are locked out until they come back in penitent mood—which they all do. Thereafter, there are frequent backslidings. But Sylvia screams and threatens, periodically refuses

175

treatment, and the backslidings become fewer and farther between. The great time to complete the dietary education of a Hollywood movie girl is during one of those interludes (they all pass through them) when the last picture contract is dead and the new one hasn't been offered. Then, living on credit, running up bills, frightened, chastened, ready to listen to reason, the over-size babies can be taught something. In the long run, invariably, the knowledge is finally appreciated. *Good dieting is good eating.* When they find that out, the boss has done all she can do for a patient. Good-by patient.

The proposition, here, is to sum up Sylvia's diet knowledge as it was brought to bear on the people of Part One, taking them in the order of their appearance in these pages. As will become apparent as we go along, the boss handles diet problems from a dual point of view: the elements of the diet, and their preparation. Of the two, the latter is *much the more important.* A pork chop, properly cooked, would be a much better diet dish than a chicken wing fried in fat and ignorance. The place where the chemistry, quality and suitability of your food is decided is *not* in a scientific tract setting forth the calorie, protein, vitamin contents of this and that raw product; it is *not* in the package from the patent food manufacturer; it is *not* in test-tubes, treatises and tabulated statistics; it *is* over the burner of your kitchen range. There you may negotiate the miracle of your physical regeneration. There also, you may concoct an assortment of deadly poisons from the evil effects of which not even Sylvia's fists, pounding at their merriest, can deliver you.

2. MARIE DRESSLER'S "AS IS" DIET

MARIE DRESSLER, as has been told, went through a period in Hollywood when, for business reasons, she put up a million-dollar front. By way of awing the financial executives of a company which was

177

trying desperately to circumscribe her salary demands, she set up a semi-royal establishment in a
turreted castle of the Hollywood hills. An unex-
pected result of this purely political maneuver
was that idleness, plus a Filipino cook with an
oriental imagination, began to tell on her mid-
section. Sylvia had to put her foot down.

In the long run, Sylvia and Marie Dressler
worked out a sort of compromise, Miss Dressler put
in the claim that, being a middle-aged woman, stout
(and what of it?), she wanted to remain about as
was—healthy, but comfortable. Sylvia conceded
the point and the result was what you might call the
"As Is," or

MARIE DRESSLER DIET

(*A Characteristic Day*)

BREAKFAST
1 small glass of orange juice
2 thin slices of crisp bacon
1 soft-boiled egg
1 cup of coffee with 1 lump of sugar,
    little cream

178

DIET AND WHOLESOME COOKING

LUNCHEON

1 cup of consommé
1 mixed fruit salad, no dressing
1 broiled lamb chop
3 heaping tablespoons of carrots
2 heaping tablespoons of fresh peas
1 small glass of fruit jello
1 cup of tea with lemon

DINNER

1 cup of broth
1 seafood cocktail
2 thin slices of roast beef
20 stalks of thin green asparagus
Fresh fruit (no bananas)
Demitasse coffee

You're not going to catch me, nor the boss either, recommending the above plot of a day's eating as the final word on eating to keep fit. Neither Marie Dressler nor any other human being who isn't a nut and a food faddist is going to pick out any one of the diet menus listed herein and stick to it. There was a fad a few years ago for doping out a menu and making it do for every day

179

of the week. But anybody who will eat the same food, day after day, week after week, is unnatural and probably a chess player.

The fact is, you can't hand out a diet, because that would involve doping out 365 menus per person, to take care of the variations of individual types and of the necessity for variety in anybody's eating. The best we can do is to give a sample diet day in each star's case and hope that nobody will get the idea, for instance, that during the time Sylvia bossed her eating, Marie Dressler ate one hundred and twenty consecutive dinners all beginning with "one cup of broth" and ending with "fresh fruit (no bananas)."

One thing I can do that will teach 99 per cent of you something you don't know, and that is tell you how to *cook* the items on your diet list—any diet list.

Strictly between you and me, pretty nearly *all* diets that get published are equally good, the diet doped out by Dr. Whoozis for the morning paper being no better nor worse than the diet figured out

180

DIET AND WHOLESOME COOKING

for the evening paper by Mehitabel Menu. The factor that licks dietitians and makes them look like saps to the lady that follows all the instructions and still sticks at 300 pounds is that there isn't one person in a thousand who knows how to do so simple a thing as grill a lamb chop without turning it into something I wouldn't feed to the boss's cat.

BROILING

(1) To get good meat (as anyone knows) you select the chop or steak that, on the butcher's counter, shows the most fat.

(2) BUT, *before broiling,* you cut out said fat with a knife. That's elemental.

(3) Your oven being red-hot, you present the piece of meat to the flame in such a way that the fats which are burned out drip into a receptacle below the meat and several inches away from it; the idea being that the meat must *not* cook in its own juices.

(4) The quicker the cooking, the better. Unless you have an aversion to rare meat, eat your

chop or steak blood-red inside and burnt outside.

(5) Do *not* undo all you have done to make the meat digestible and non-fattening by proceeding now to pour back over it the fats which have collected in the catch-pan. If you must have a sauce, serve it with a small lump of fresh butter placed on the meat as it goes to table. This element of *timing* is important because, whereas fresh melted butter is harmless in small quantities, *cooked* butter is unwholesome and is excluded from all diets.

(6) While we're on the subject of meat, let me add a remark intended as a loud and raucous snort in the direction of all the diet quacks who continually add to the sum of their own and the public's ignorance by handing out hooey about "meatless diets." Meat is a necessary part of any reducing diet. Meat does not fatten, if properly selected and prepared. And when a person is following a reducing diet, meat is *absolutely imperative*, because reducing diets have a tendency to weaken, which can only be combated by good red meat. Broiled or roasted, all cuts of beef and the

182

prime cuts of lamb are first-rate diet items. Meats should *never* be fried and most of them are deteriorated by boiling. An exception to the last is boiled ham. In refutation of the common assumption that pork is harmful, cold *boiled* ham stands at the head of the list of meats (even above broiled beef) which are easily assimilable by the touchiest digestive tracts.

3. THE MAE MURRAY DIET

(*Maybe Somebody Will Try It; She Wouldn't*)

BREAKFAST
1 small glass of grapefruit juice
1 slice of wholewheat toast
1 glass of skimmed milk
1 cup of coffee, clear

LUNCHEON
1 cup of broth
1 slice of broiled calf's liver
3 heaping tablespoons of spinach
1 small baked potato
1 cup of custard with 1 spoonful
    of fruit juice
1 cup of tea clear

183

HOLLYWOOD UNDRESSED

DINNER

1 fruit cocktail
1 cup of vegetable soup
1 small broiled steak
3 heaping tablespoons of carrots
3 heaping tablespoons of fresh peas
1 small dish of fresh berries
1 glass of skimmed milk
1 demitasse of coffee

AGAIN the remark is made that this is necessarily a sample day taken from many and that there is no virtue in a monotonous code of eating.

And again it is stressed that the most valuable data that can be given by a dietitian who does not personally supervise the patient have to do with not so much *what* is to be eaten as *how* it should be prepared. From the above menu, then, let's take the item, vegetable soup. Oh, *you* know how to make a thing so simple and common as vegetable soup. Yes, you do! Any bets?

VEGETABLE SOUP

Every day of the year, American housewives, twenty million of them, throw away as waste-matter

184

at least fifty per cent of the food bought with hard-earned cash when they empty out as useless the waters in which vegetables are cooked. The same cook who hoards meat remnants and bones like a dog and keeps a meat-stock pot on the back of her stove, cheerfully tosses into the sink the better part of the food values of vegetables. It would be *less foolish* to throw away the vegetables and keep the liquid in which they were cooked. Vegetables should be boiled in just enough water to prevent burning— no more. The combined waters in which the vegetables for a day's meals have been boiled, when put in a common container and reduced by further boiling, make a valuable light vegetable broth just as is and can be thickened with such adjuncts as sago, tapioca, winter squash or vermicelli, seasoned and served without further ado. Or

(1) Obtain from your grocer a "soup bunch" consisting of all the vegetables *and salad greens* in season; the cost should average twenty-five cents.

(2) Add to these three medium-sized Irish

185

potatoes and one medium turnip (more turnip will make the soup bitter); also add all available rough greens, such as turnip-, celery- and beet-tops.

(3) Shred the greens. Dice the vegetables in ½-inch cubes.

(4) Immerse the mass in twice its volume of the vegetable stock described in paragraph 1 or in plain water.

(5) Bring to a boil. Reduce the heat and let simmer for two or three hours, adding water from time to time to make up for loss through evaporation.

(6) Strain, add small amount of salt, serve hot or cold.

4. THE MARY DUNCAN DIET

(A Diet for Adolescent Girls Inclined to Plumpness)

BREAKFAST
½ grapefruit
2 slices of crisp rye toast with thin butter
1 cup of coffee, clear

DIET AND WHOLESOME COOKING

½ canteloupe
1 broiled lamb chop
4 heaping tablespoonfuls of cauliflower
2 heaping tablespoonfuls of summer squash
2 leaves of lettuce
3 slices of tomato, diet dressing
½ slice of wholewheat toast, no butter
1 cup of coffee, clear

DINNER

1 tomato-juice cocktail
Russian salad, diet dressing
1 slice of roast beef or 2 slices of roast
      lamb—"lean" gravy
3 heaping tablespoons of spinach
2 heaping tablespoons of Brussels sprouts
½ slice of wholewheat toast
1 small dish of strawberries
1 glass of skimmed milk
Demitasse coffee

IT's the first time a roast has appeared on one of these diet menus and, as in the case of the grilled chop, I suppose you think you know how to roast meat. Maybe you do, maybe you don't. The chances are you don't follow the procedure below—the only

187

correct one for the preparation of non-fattening roast meat.

(1) As in the case of the lamb chop, you naturally choose a good tender fattish roast off the butcher's counter, buying the best meat. Again you cut out all the visible pieces of fat when you're preparing the roast for the pan, which should have deep furrows in the bottom to catch the drippings.

(2) Season with very little salt (salt is fattening) and some pepper.

(3) Get the oven red hot.

(4) Figure on roasting 15 to 20 minutes per pound.

(5) When the outside of the roast is browned, you baste. But *do not* baste with the drippings. Baste with a cup of hot water, operating slowly and drenching especially the spots where there are outcroppings of fat.

(6) When the roast is done, remove it from the pan. Now take the pan of drippings and pour into it a half-cup of boiling water. Until the pan

DIET AND WHOLESOME COOKING

cools, keep skimming off the fat that rises to the top of the water.

(7) What is left in the pan is now a pure blood juice with very little fat. Heated up again, it may be served, *without thickening of any kind,* with the roast. Or in the form of the jelly which it will take on cooling, it may be served in strips with the cold roast.

This method of preparing a roast removes fats so successfully that a fresh ham roast can be served on diet menus if the cooking has been carefully done.

5. TWO DIETS OF LAWRENCE TIBBETT'S

A SINGER has a diet problem more delicate than that of the most fragile girl. It is necessary that a singer never perform while the stomach is full. Therefore the last solid meal before a performance is taken about 5 P.M., giving the stomach time to empty before curtain hour. This throws the whole

189

time-table of eating off-center, as the "performance-day" diet in the left-hand column below shows. The diet is a special one, occupational rather than remedial—Tibbett having little about his strong physique that needs remedy! The diets are not Sylvia's, but were written out for her by Mr. Tibbett, who can recommend them to other professional singers and to those ordinary citizens who occasionally have to give banquet speeches or do other vocal stunts and need a tip about how to face the ordeal in at least a good physical condition.

BREAKFAST

Part of glass of grapefruit juice ½ hour before breakfast

When Singing	*Not Singing*
2 poached eggs	All-fruit breakfast (fresh
Thin buttered whole wheat	figs or any fresh fruit in
toast	season)
Crisp bacon	1 glass of warm milk
Warm milk	

LUNCHEON

No luncheon	Avocado salad
	Wholewheat toast

190

DIET AND WHOLESOME COOKING

DINNER

(*On a night when Mr. Tib-bett has to sing an operatic rôle he dines about five hours before time to sing*)

Purée of spinach

Fresh peas

2 lamb chops

Head of lettuce with dressing of Italian olive oil, lemon and salt

Thin wholewheat toast

1 glass of milk

(*A favorite dinner on a night when Mr. Tibbett is not singing*)

Avocado cocktail, Thousand Island dressing

Plain tomato soup with celery, no crackers

Rare roast beef

Potatoes, mashed with cream and butter

Corn on cob

Toast, no coffee

Combination salad—tomatoes, water cress, romaine, celery, onion, cucumber, raw carrots, raw cabbage — and mayonnaise

Blackberry or peach cobbler

LAWRENCE TIBBETT's menus hardly belong here because they're certainly not for diet meals. Avocado salad and peach cobbler! M-mh. But Tibbett has the constitution of a wolf and can probably digest leather.

191

Eggs are mentioned here for the first time and will not be listed in any of the diets prescribed by Sylvia.

The reason is not that a *fresh egg* can't find a place in the strictest diet. But the chances are so slim that you'll ever get a supply of fresh eggs that Sylvia has had to exclude them rather than expose her clients to the risks of eating stale hen-fruit.

An egg *less* than twenty-four hours old is an excellent, nourishing, easily assimilable item of food. But an egg *over* twenty-four hours old is just the reverse. The egg-dealers in America have produced a situation that would not be tolerated except by a nation of saps. It is practically impossible to obtain an egg that has not lain in cold-storage for anywhere from ten weeks to ten years. If it were generally understood that eggs *must* be eaten within 24 hours of their laying or not at all, then the egg distributors would have to organize the way the milk dealers have done.

If you can get eggs specially delivered from

the country, eat them boiled three to four minutes,
or poached. Otherwise, lay off!

6. THE INA CLAIRE DIET

(Overweight plus Anemia)

BREAKFAST

Small glass grapefruit juice
2 tablespoonfuls of one of the baked patent
    cereals with a glass of skimmed milk
Tea, one lump of sugar

LUNCHEON

Salad of cottage cheese with shredded pine-
    apple, no dressing
Cup of broth with liver extract (hot or jellied)
2 tablespoonfuls of carrots, 2 of spinach and
    1 of peas
Apple mold

DINNER

Celery
Sweetbreads with truffles
3 heaping spoonfuls of string beans, 2 of sum-
    mer squash
Tomato jelly, diet dressing
Stewed fruit
Black coffee

INA CLAIRE'S was a special diet, at once reducing and strengthening. There was a definite debility to be considered, as she was inclined to anemia. Somewhere I have already mentioned that meat should be a regular part of all reducing diets, to offset the possible weakening effect of cutting down on rations. As Miss Claire's trouble is a widespread one, especially among women, a reducing diet for anemic persons overweight should be helpful.

DIET DRESSING in connection with salads has been repeated several times without explanation. It is simply a healthy substitute for the classic French dressing, with which it is contrasted below.

French Dressing	Diet Dressing
Olive oil	Mineral oil
Vinegar	Lemon juice
Salt and pepper	The same (but as little salt as possible, salt being fattening)

IF your state of health warrants using an oil other than mineral, you will still do well to avoid olive

194

oil, the heavy and indigestible element of French dressing. The French themselves have universally adopted oil of arrachide (a Sahara desert plant) as a substitute for olive oil and their olive oil industry survives on export to America and on the demands of the soap manufacturers.

LIVER EXTRACT, mentioned above, can be prepared in the kitchen by chopping up cow's liver, covering with cold water, bringing to a boil and simmering for three to four hours. (There is a patent product which cannot be named here which is superior to the home-made liver extract.) The brew obtained from the liver is combined, half and half, with the broth of vegetables or meat, and is the element of the diet which is the most effective counter-agent against anemia.

7. THE GLORIA SWANSON DIET

PROPERLY, one cannot give a "Gloria Swanson Diet." Gloria's case was complex, and so was the matter of her diet. At first she had to be overfed,

195

as part of the treatment of her run-down nervous condition. She was never sentenced to one of the drastic reducing diets. In her case, ample nourishment had to be kept up and the reducing part of the program had to be provided by mechanical means —which was to say massage in her case. If you are nervous and run-down and, as a consequence, overweight, do not risk any of the hundred percent reducing diets listed herein, but use vigorous exercise and massage as correctives of the increase of weight which would otherwise be bound to result from the long hours of sleep you need and at least one daily meal as copious and strengthening as the second one below.

(Typical Meals for Nourishing the Nerves While Causing No Increase in Weight)

BREAKFAST-LUNCHEON
Half grapefruit
Small dish of fresh figs
3 slices of calf's liver
2 slices of crisp rye toast with **thin butter**
1 dish of fresh raspberries, plain
Cup of tea, one lump of sugar

DIET AND WHOLESOME COOKING

D I N N E R
Broth
Roast pheasant or chicken; or boiled fish
2 tablespoons of mashed turnips
2 tablespoons of string beans
 (or substitute two scoops of noodles with
 melted butter for one of these)
Pickled beets
Sherbet
Black coffee

NOODLES. The diet food value of noodles has
never been adequately published in America. In
Europe the diet uses of this starchy but non-
fattening food are well-known. When eaten as the
sole starch item of a diet, noodles not only do not
fatten, but are directly healing in many cases where
an irritated condition of the digestive tract exists.

The only noodles to use are the plain Italian
wheat-noodles, without any flavoring ingredients.
Egg-noodles are debarred. Naturally, all the spa-
ghetti sauces are excluded as they are all mixtures
harmfully concocted in pans of frying fat.

Cook the noodles not less than ten, *not more*
197

than twenty minutes (the time given on the average package is correct). Have the water boiling and *slightly* salted from the start.

Serve as soon as ready, under a pat of fresh butter which melts on the way to the table.

The positive virtue of noodles as a food for sufferers from colitis or kindred intestinal complaints is in the fact that they form a poultice for the irritated tissues and digest without strain.

FRYING. Reference to "frying fat" is made above and the Swanson diet includes *boiled* fish. Here, then, is the place to say that there is only one rule about frying: DON'T! This is a rule not only of dietary but of all sane cooking. Fried foods are certainly the origin of the chronic digestive troubles which identify the native American (by his belch!) to doctors all over the world. *There is nothing that should be fried.* And if you're lazy, and don't like to hear this, and if you forget it between now and dinner, which is to be prepared as usual in the quick-and-easy pan of grease—why,

198

go ahead. Suit yourself, only don't go squealing to your doctor or your masseuse and say you don't know how it is you have so much stomach trouble, for you greased yourself for the skid.

As fish can no more be fried than any other food, they must be boiled or grilled. Buy only the "lean" varieties of fish. By lean fish are meant those of the trout family, pike, *true* sole (unobtainable in America) and a few others showing no fat between skin and flesh. Boiled (but not so long as to soften the firm flesh) these are all excellent, with melted butter. The lean fish are less satisfactory broiled as that method of cooking accentuates the natural dryness.

8. THE CONSTANCE BENNETT DIET

Fattening

The diet below is the only fattening diet herein. Meals similar to these will build up your weight, but not at the expense of your health.

HOLLYWOOD UNDRESSED

BREAKFAST

Glass of orange juice

Dish of hominy mixed with one over-ripe
sliced banana with cream and sugar

Glass of certified milk (half milk, half cream)

LUNCHEON

Half avocado (alligator pear) on lettuce with
mayonnaise (made in your own kitchen)

3 heaping tablespoons of turnips en purée

3 heaping tablespoons of fresh green peas

2 slices of wholewheat toast with plenty of
fresh butter

1 dish stewed fruit

1 glass certified milk

DINNER

1 cup creamed fresh tomato soup

Mixed grill of lamb chops, kidneys, two strips
of crisp bacon

Beets in fresh melted butter (melted by the
heat of the served dish)

Mashed potatoes

Cup of custard, vanilla sauce (the egg for the
custard to be less than one day old)

Black coffee

STEWED FRUIT. Fruit is stewed when there is any reason for avoiding raw foods. Raw foods are stricken from the diets of persons suffering from colitis or kindred disarrangements of the intestinal tract. Whenever you feel "out of sorts" you will do well to cut out raw foods from your diet.

When you stew fruit, do not cook the fruit until it is shapeless and tasteless. Follow this plan:

1. Cook the fruit whole, except those that must be peeled and cored.

2. Cover with cold sugared water.

3. Bring to a boil. Then take off the fire immediately and cool.

When you are on the non-raw food régime, salads are also cooked. Lettuce and the other edible leaves are immersed in boiling water for two minutes and served as a vegetable.

9. SYLVIA'S DIET LORE

(Diet fads come, diet fads go, but one thing never changes: the art of diet cooking)

MEAT

Pay no attention to meatless diet fads.

Broil or roast the leaner meats in such a way as to eliminate the fats, first by cutting away the visible excess before cooking and, second, by taking the measures I have described for eliminating contact between meats and their drippings.

Do not boil meats. However, you may eat cold boiled ham as often as you wish.

FISH

In contradistinction to meats, fish should be boiled. Only the lean varieties should be used.

VEGETABLES

Should be boiled or steamed in only as much water as will prevent burning and should be cooked no longer than is necessary to make them palatable.

The better parts of vegetables being absorbed in the cooking waters, preserve all of these for making the pure vegetable broths and soups you should habitually eat.

202

DIET AND WHOLESOME COOKING

BUTTER

Harmless in small quantities if *never* cooked. Therefore
butter should always be added to hot dishes with
which it is served just before they go to the table.
Sweet butter is best, and can always be obtained in
Jewish stores.

EGGS

Dangerous on account of American distribution methods
which provide the public with stale eggs. To be
used only when they are certified to be not more
than 24 hours old. Soft boiled, poached or incor-
porated in custards.

FRUIT

With the exception of certain berries which disagree
with particular constitutions, all are excellent. However, when there is reason to suspect disorders of the
digestive tract, they should be stewed, though not
longer than it takes the sugared water to come to
a boil.

CONDIMENTS, SAUCES

Always to be suspected. Salt fattens. Peppers, mustard,
etc. are indigestible. Any sauce which has been fried
is vile. Prefer mineral and neutral vegetable oils to
olive oil. For vinegar substitute lemon juice. Avoid
cocktail sauces with the exception of the plain and
pure juices which are erroneously called cocktails.

HOLLYWOOD UNDRESSED

SEA FOODS

With the exception of "lean" fish, they are generally to
be avoided—especially the crustaceans.

NOODLES

Despite their starch content, they are non-fattening when
eaten plain-boiled with melted butter. Helpful in all
conditions involving irritation of the digestive tract.

And now to conclude with a diet day recommended to all who suffer from digestive disorders.
If your digestive apparatus is on the blink, either
because of disease or because of an excess, try
living on this fare for a few days.

A MID-DAY DINNER

Vegetable broth
Cold boiled ham
Noodles boiled 10 to 20 minutes (follow instructions on the package) and served
with a pat of butter
Stewed fruit

SUPPER

Clabber and hot or cold boiled potatoes (lots
of clabber and little potato)
Stewed fruit

204

~~~~~~

II

OVERWEIGHT AND THE GLANDS

THE BOSS has helped me out of a tough spot here. I asked about the causes and treatment of overweight and underweight when it's not something so simple and easily detectable as the patient's over-indulgences. Well, Sylvia wasn't to be lured into shooting off her mouth about the new science of the endocrine glands, with which the doctors propose eventually to handle the great number of cases of obesity and under-development due to a deep-seated cause which no amount of massage, exercise, or even diet, can reach.

After several days Sylvia turned over to me

205

a paper on the subject prepared by R—— M——, M.D., of Hollywood.* Here is a digest.

Roughly, people take on weight for two reasons: either because there is bad balance between their intake of fuel (food) and their expenditure of energy (work); or because of metabolic disturbances resulting in a derangement of their normal physiology and biochemistry. In many cases both causes are present.

Bad eating habits, lack of physical activity, may be simply corrected. The results of these sins of omission and commission may be banished by diet and mechanical means, by which is meant exercise, sweating, massage.

But those who are overweight through maladjustments of the organism—these must be handled by competent medical advisors.

By far the most important and probably the

* In keeping with a traditional stand against personal advertising, the American Medical Association, of which he is a member and Los Angeles delegate, advises Dr. R—— M——, our expert, against use of his name in connection with a lay publication. Dr. M—— has kindly volunteered to answer any medical questions that his words raise in your mind. He can be addressed, care of the publishers.

most prevalent type in this second class are those whose obesity is due to deficiencies of the glands of internal secretion. Their condition is truly pathological, either congenital or acquired, and necessitates intensive treatment.

The causes of endocrine upsets may be spontaneous but frequently follow acute infections such as influenza, etc., or to physiological changes in other glands (mumps is particularly dangerous). The commonest example is obesity following pregnancy. The pituitary, thyroid, mammary and other glands are normally overactive during pregnancy; while the ovaries are quiescent—a very natural compensatory adjustment. Following delivery, with the return of the function of the ovaries, these other glands sometimes fail to return to normal, continue overactive for a while, and then exhaust themselves. It is obvious that the problem here is to determine which gland is primarily at fault and which is secondary. The reëstablishment of an "endrocine balance" is the aim.

The offending gland is usually the thyroid or

pituitary, the latter much more frequently than was suspected a few years ago. The pituitary is about the size of a pea and is located between the eyes opposite the temples and beneath the point where the optic nerves cross. The gland has two major portions: the anterior lobe, controlling the bone, muscle and genital development during youth and functioning in maintenance of strength in adult life; and the posterior lobe, controlling fat metabolism, tone of smooth muscles, etc. Overactivities of the anterior lobe during the years of development cause freaks such as giants, etc. Overactivity of the posterior lobe causes high blood pressure, loss of weight, etc. Conversely, underactivity of the anterior lobe results in deficiencies and the adult turns out a weakling; while underactivity of the posterior lobe results in obesity. Terrific frontal headaches are the outstanding symptoms of pituitary gland trouble, and there may be optical disturbances.

The thyroid gland is of equal importance in

the body to the pituitary, although probably secondary as regards obesity. It is composed of two lobes the size of oysters situated on either side of the "wind-pipe" at the level of the "collar bones" and connected by an isthmus of gland. Children born with thyroid deficiencies are apt to be mentally defective, show faulty teeth, bones and muscular development. The normal gland supplies a hormone—"thyroxin"—which influences carbohydrate metabolism. Friendly in normal conditions, this thyroxin is very poisonous when produced in excess. It precipitates goitres of various kinds and produces symptoms of nervousness, loss of weight, heart palpitations and all manner of toxic phenomena. A harmless type of thyroid enlargement often appears at puberty, especially in girls, in certain parts of the country where there is not enough iodine in the water supply. Underactivity of the thyroid produces effects opposed to all the above. Among these, and along with mental sluggishness, constant fatigue, anemia, kidney trouble, is obesity. Many other glands of internal secretion are contained in the body, including the gonads, adrenals, pancreas, parathyroids, thymus, mammary and the pineal. There are also problematical endocrine functions of the liver, spleen, prostate and lymphatic glands. The interrelationships among all these is very complex.

The factor of the endocrines in obesity is established and is recognized more and more by the general public. The medical profession is conducting a tremendous amount of research in this promising field and vast stores of scientific information are being accumulated for the aid of the present and future generations.

Your family doctor is ready to apply much of this information to your particular case, if you are over- or under-weight. I earnestly recommend that your first step toward recovering your normal (and well-balanced) condition be a visit to him. Certainly, if you have experimented with mechanical and surface measures and have further gone through a program of such dieting as you have

OVERWEIGHT AND THE GLANDS

selected from the reams of advice shoved at the masses by all and sundry—if you have done all this without results, then at least do yourself the justice of seeking out competent medical help.

‏〰〰〰〰〰〰〰〰〰〰〰〰〰〰〰〰〰〰〰〰〰

III

YOUR MEASUREMENTS AND
THEIR REMEDIES

I N A MAD world, common sense has all the values of originality. For me, the boss's dope on diets sticks out of the run of such stuff like a pair of sane eyes in a psycopathic ward.

The same, if you'll agree with me, applies to the system of measurements and exercises Sylvia uses in her work-shop. The usual thing is to chart the measurements of some peerless beauty—usually a professional who works at beauty like Bobby Jones at golf—and tell the amateur who asks for advice:

YOUR MEASUREMENTS

"Take a look at this Venus. Wherever you're different from her, you're wrong. See the cashier on the way out."

It's obvious that a woman's measurements should agree *relatively*—that is, with respect to one another—not with those of some standard type, arbitrarily selected, anywhere from an inch to a foot taller or shorter than the poor sucker who nevertheless breaks her heart and her back trying to achieve somebody else's waistline. This is obvious. Sylvia's "percent" table of correct measurements says it in a form which is generally applicable to a six-foot Juno or a five-foot cutie and the assorted sizes in between.

1. WHAT YOU SHOULD MEASURE

A BIT of study and use of the chart on the following page will probably make it self-explanatory. However, a line on the method of operation may not be amiss.

(See page 216.)

HOLLYWOOD UNDRESSED

CORRECT MEASUREMENTS

Using the girth of the hips as the basis of her system, Sylvia has worked out an ideal table of measurements. There are also given here the actual measurements of two well-proportioned girls—Alice White and Mary Duncan.

	IDEAL MEASUREMENTS	ALICE WHITE'S MEASUREMENTS	MARY DUNCAN'S MEASUREMENTS
NECK.......	Hip-Girth $\times$ 0.36	11½ in.	12½ in.
UPPER ARM..	Hip-Girth $\times$ 0.30	9½ in.	10½ in.
WRIST.......	Hip-Girth $\times$ 0.175	5½ in.	6 in.
CHEST......	Hip-Girth $\times$ 0.98	30 in.	33¼ in.
WAIST......	Hip-Girth $\times$ 0.76	23 in.	26 in.
THIGH......	Hip-Girth $\times$ 0.60	19 in.	20 in.
CALF.......	Hip-Girth $\times$ 0.36	11¼ in.	12½ in.
ANKLE......	Hip-Girth $\times$ 0.23	7¼ in.	8 in.
HEIGHT.....	Hip-Girth $\times$ 1.90	5 ft.	5 ft. 4½ in.

214

YOUR MEASUREMENTS

MEASUREMENTS OF LENGTH

These are all plumb-line measurements, with the height (hip-girth × 1.90) as the basis. The best way to get plumb-line measurements is to mark each point against the wall. The tape-measure or rule then gives you true measurements without possibility of error due to the curves of the body.

	IDEAL MEASUREMENTS	ALICE WHITE'S MEASUREMENTS	MARY DUNCAN'S MEASUREMENTS
LOWER LEG..... Height × 0.31		18½ in.	20 in.
(Heel to top of knee-cap)			
THIGH........ Height × 0.33		19½ in.	24¼ in.
(Top of knee-cap to top of hip-bone)			
TORSO........ Height × 0.235		14½ in.	15¼ in.
(Hip line to chin point)			
HEAD.......... Height × 0.125		7½ in.	8 in.
Total.............. 1.000		60 in.	64½ in.

215

First: You don't know how to do a decimal multiplication? You ought to be ashamed of yourself. Get some school-child of your acquaintance to help you.

Second: Sylvia chooses the hip measurement as the basis for her calculations because, with all its damnable fluctuations, it is still the nearest thing to a constant girth-measurement in the body, being built around a massive core of bone. Also, it is the largest girth measurement of the normal female body.

Third: As to the chart's application to yourself. Let's assume that, having measured your hips, your tape-measure tells you they are 36 inches around. Consulting the chart, you find that the circumference of your neck should be 36% of that of your hips. The answer is 36 times .36 equals 12.96. Your neck, therefore, should measure about 13 inches around. This will be *your* neck—not Mary Duncan's neck, or the Venus de Milo's neck, but your very own and the neck that will best become you.

216

YOUR MEASUREMENTS

You will want to know if your horizontal measurements are in keeping with your height. Sylvia gives the multiplicator (190%) by which the height that goes with your hips is calculated: 36 times 1.90 is 68.4 inches. Your height should be 5 feet 8½ inches.

If you work through the list of measurements and find that your theoretical answers, derived from the percentage table, are hopelessly at variance with the facts, there is but one answer: you started off with the wrong figure—you have not the hips that belong to you and something has got to be done about it. On the other hand, if your height is three or four inches under double the girth of your hips, but some of the other theoretical measurements are radically different from the facts, you have spotted local imperfections—of chest, waist, thigh, etc.—and are informed of the approximate number of inches by which they are under- or over-developed.

As for weight measurements—Sylvia has discarded them entirely, has thrown the bathroom scales out of the work-room and advises her patients to do the same at home. Of two women of equal height, both in prime condition, both showing approximately the same (correct) tape-measurements, one may be large-boned and compact and weigh ten pounds more than the other, small-boned and soft-fleshed. The weighing scales are very arbitrary and unintelligent critics of your person and should not be consulted seriously. Patients come to the boss for reducing, are beaten into shape, prove it to themselves with the tape-measure and then are astounded (and usually dismayed) to find they have lost practically no weight at all. The answer is that gasses and fluids collect in pockets in the tissues and, without materially increasing the weight, are responsible for the majority of unsightly inflations which bring patients yammering into our reception room. Watch your inches, not your pounds. Stick to the tape-measure.

2. EXERCISES

You have worked out your table of ideal measurements from the chart, have found the spots that need attention, and want to do something about it.

The trouble, Sylvia has found, is that exercises and calisthenics are so deadly dull to the majority of individuals that the program of self-improvement is seldom carried out. With her patients, Sylvia has worked out and uses a series of calisthenics in duet. Pairing off patients who are neighbors, or friends, the boss has found that the work is done better. It is therefore suggested that you inveigle a girl friend into collaborating with you on your program of reducing exercises.

For the sake of clarity in the descriptions of Sylvia's routine of reducing exercises in twos, let's call girl No. 1 (the active exerciser) Beulah; girl No. 2 (the helping hand) Araminta.

EXERCISE NO. 1

BEULAH stands erect, legs comfortably separated, the feet turned slightly inward. She raises her arms full-length above her head, the palms outward. Keeping the arms parallel, stretched but not rigid,

219

and keeping her mind on the requirement that the muscles of the underarms are to be pulled until the strain can be felt, Beulah starts to sway from the waist. She has started, say, to sway to the right.

During all this time, Araminta has been reading a book or looking out the window, or selling oil stocks by telephone. But she has not forgotten that, at a crucial moment, her intrusion into Beulah's effort is required. That moment is at hand! Advancing to face the exerciser, Araminta encourages and directs Beulah's right-sway as follows: placing the palm of her left hand firmly against Beulah's right side, just above the hipbone, Araminta places her right palm against Beulah's left arm. Pushing with the right hand and resisting with the left, Araminta forces Beulah to bend as far to the right as she will go without breaking.

This swaying exercise, of course, is done to the left, alternating with the right. Five times, right and left, are enough. The effect is magical on any accumulations of fat along the under-arms, the ribs and the waist above the hip-bones.

The exercise has a variant, or an extension, which will also take off folds of fat over the hips. The swaying movement having been carried to its extreme, as above, Beulah turns slightly at the waist, in the direction of the sway, and, "breaking" at the waist, swings her shoulders and arms downward until the tips of the fingers touch the outside of her foot.

This sequence of motions is to be preferred to the popular and traditional exercise consisting in bending *forward* to touch the toes. To a woman fighting fat over the stomach, this old-fashioned movement is actually harmful. Bending like a jack-knife breaks down the fat across the waist-line, nowhere else. The result is very apt to be two stomachs instead of one. Also, this movement develops the buttocks handsomely. Dangerous fore and aft, this exercise should be avoided.

221

EXERCISE NO. 2

BEULAH (who is getting all the best of it) now crosses the room to a closed door and stands facing it, her toes against it. She rises on tip-toes and, raising her arms over her head, palms against the wall above the door, seeks to stretch herself to the furthest limit of her elasticity. When that limit has seemingly been reached, Beulah can always get another inch or two of stretch by "crawling" upward along the wall with her finger-tips.

Araminta now steps behind Beulah, facing the latter's back, and crouching slightly, seizes Beulah's arms in her hands. Araminta gets her purchase of the thick parts of Beulah's arms, just above the arm-pits and so applies the grip as to be prepared to resist any effort by Beulah to sink down on her heels. Nevertheless, this is the effort Beulah makes. She sinks slowly downward. Araminta opposes the downward trend of Beulah by pushing upward with might and main. The whole exercise is done as slowly as possible.

YOUR MEASUREMENTS

The exercise is beneficial to both participants. Beulah's lower abdomen is flattened and Araminta's waist-muscles are tautened and the efforts of both are effective in stretching and melting any accumulations of fat in the necks, shoulders and upper arms.

Sylvia prescribes the exercise (insofar as the description deals with Beulah) for women affected by child-birth. These matrons can use this exercise without fear of strain.

EXERCISE NO. 3

(For the lower half of the body: waist, thighs, legs.)

BEULAH lies on her back on the floor, feet together, arms outstretched behind her head, thumbs touching, the whole body stretched. Araminta kneels beside her partner, just opposite Beulah's knees and, placing cupped hands over Beulah's leg-muscles, just above the knees, bears down with all her weight, thus pinning Beulah's legs to the floor. So held, Beulah flings herself upward and for-

223

ward, keeping the arms always outstretched over the head, and passing through the sitting position, continues the motion forward until the fingers touch the toes.

The second movement of this exercise is the complement of the first. Beulah having returned to the initial prone position, outstretched, Araminta kneels about opposite Beulah's ribs. Beulah now raises her legs from the hips, taking care not to bend them at the knees, and, as her legs reach vertical, Araminta hooks an arm under them and forces them to continue in their arc, until the toes touch the floor back of Beulah's head.

All of the above exercises can be done without strain by the beginner five times at each session. Later, they may be done as many as ten times— never more; excessive exercise is bad for women.

THESE three exercise sequences will keep most of the body in good condition. In fact, only two parts of the body are unaffected by them: the face and the breasts. The care of the face, of course, will be the subject of another chapter.

THE BREASTS. As for the breasts, they cannot be safely submitted to *any* kind of direct mechanical treatment. A great many women today are paying the penalty imposed on them some years ago by what was a persistent style in dress, calling for a flat-chested effect. Many will remember the compressing devices used during the period to give women the unnatural boyish appearance. In relaxed and deteriorated muscles of the bust and chest, many of Sylvia's patients now show the disastrous effects of the fad.

Sylvia is obliged to tell these women that their only recourse is a drastic diet, systematically followed. Every second hour of the day, drink six ounces of any liquid food—fruit juices, buttermilk, skimmed milk, tomato juice. Continue this regimen for three days running, taking no other nourishment whatever during the period. Two weeks later, go on a three-day liquid diet again. Repeat patiently until the breasts are reduced. It

225

is a long, slow process. When the reduction begins to show, there will probably be a tendency to flabbiness. If so, gently rub in a double-strength solution of spirits of camphor, which will tighten up the skin. . . . Plastic surgery reports some successful work in cases of over-development or flabbiness of the breasts.

For developing the breasts there is only one course which may possibly succeed. Take up swimming and singing, with an instructor for both. Singers never complain of under-development of the chest and breasts; quite the contrary. Generally speaking, imperfections of the breasts are the most rebellious ones with which the female body can be afflicted. The professional specialists move here with the greatest caution, and doubtfully. The amateur had best not move at all, and certainly you must never have anything to do with the patent nostrums advertised as reducers or developers of the breasts. They are apt to be very injurious to the health.

The half-hour of mutual exercising having

ended, the girls may profitably conclude the session by alternating in giving each other Sylvia's once-over massage, an ankle-to-shoulder rub-down (or rather rub-up) which is imitative of professional massage, but edited here for the use of amateurs.

In this connection, it must be stressed that massage, as one of the important branches of therapeutics, is strictly a professional matter and can be dangerous if done ignorantly. Therefore you are *warned* not to deviate from or extend in any way the series of leg, back and arm manipulations described below. Above all, *never* touch the subject's abdomen or breast. Abdominal massage can only be applied by a first-rate professional, and even these let the chest and throat (with the underlying net-work of mammary and thymus glands) severely alone.

227

HOLLYWOOD UNDRESSED

3. THE RUB-UP

Beulah lies face-down on a narrow divan. She relaxes completely.

1. THE FEET

ARAMINTA, standing to one side of the divan, slips one palm under the arch of Beulah's right foot, lifts it to a convenient height, and clasps the heel with her other hand. Holding Beulah's heel immobile with one hand, Araminta continues to force the former's toes upward with the other hand, the exertion of the opposed forces resulting in doubling up the foot and stretching its arch, from ankle to toe-tips. The ligaments should be stretched quite powerfully, almost but not quite painfully.

Reverse of the above: Araminta switches her position to the foot of the divan and, grasping Beulah's right heel between palm and thumb of one hand, prepares to pull it. Simultaneously, Araminta places the palm of her other hand against the ball of Beulah's foot and pushes it. Pulling the heel and pushing the ball of Beulah's foot, Araminta stretches the tendons joining heel and calf.

Both of the above movements may be repeated five times on each foot. The line of force
which is applied must be exactly in the line of the
body of the person to whom it is applied.

2. KNOTTY OR FAT CALVES

BEULAH lies on her back.

Araminta prepares for this and subsequent
manipulations of Beulah by spreading cold-cream
on her fingers and palms and dips into the cream
jar from time to time, as her hands become dry.

Araminta stands at the foot of the divan and
grasps Beulah's right heel with her left hand, getting a firm hold with thumb and palm. With her
right hand she now administers to Beulah's right
calf the characteristic sliding and rotating manipulation of so-called Swedish massage. In this manipulation the masseuse's thumb, pointed forward
and traveling in the line of the part to be massaged, is the guide of the manipulation which is
administered by the fingers. Massage is always

toward the heart. The fingers "swim" along the surface to be massaged, alternately straightening in line with the thumb and bending away from it as this "guide" slides upward along the subject's muscle. In this case (calf-massage) the line followed by the thumb is the shin-bone.

The "crawl-stroke" movement begun, and guided along the upward line given by Beulah's shin-bone, Araminta (without stopping at Beulah's knee) shifts her position to the side of the bed and continues the stroke on upward over Beulah's thigh-muscle, guiding the massaging hand toward the hip-bone, where this phase of the rubbing ends. After a few trials, Araminta finds, to guide her hand in its course above Beulah's knee, the slight depression outlining the big thigh muscle which is anchored at the latter's hip-bone. The massaging hand should press firmly into the subject's flesh, but should not "dig" into it. This remark applies to all the massage movements.

YOUR MEASUREMENTS

3. HANDS AND ARMS

BEULAH lies on one side, facing Araminta, who stands beside the divan.

Araminta firmly grasps Beulah's right hand in her left, between palm and thumb and in such fashion that Araminta's fore-finger lies just below the line of Beulah's knuckles. Thus, Beulah's hand is held immobile, while her fingers are free to move. Araminta now seizes these bunched fingers with her free hand and "grinds" them, slowly and gently, in such a manner as to cause them to rotate slightly in their knuckle joints. From here, on to the shoulder, the "coffee-grinder" motion is applied to each arm-joint in succession—as follows:

Araminta grasps Beulah's wrist, above the joint, with one hand and, seizing Beulah's fist with her free one, rotates the whole hand gently, grinding it in the wrist sockets.

Araminta grasps Beulah's arm above the elbow and similarly "grinds" Beulah's lower arm in the elbow socket.

231

Finally, Araminta folds Beulah's arms at the elbow and, using both hands to grip Beulah's whole arm, "grinds" it in the shoulder socket.

Deposits from the blood-stream are prone to collect in the joints of the hands and arms and the above "grinding" treatment is effective in breaking up such deposits and sending them back into the blood-stream, to be carried off to some other dumping ground.

To finish off the treatment of the arm, Araminta now takes Beulah's hand in a firm grasp and, stretching Beulah's arm to the full, applies along its whole length, from wrist to shoulder, the "crawl-stroke" treatment described for treatment of the leg. The path of the guiding thumb here is, first, the inside of the forearm up to the elbow; then a diagonal past the inside of the elbow joint to the outside of the upper-arm and then between the bone and the biceps on up to the shoulder joint. Reaching the shoulder joint, Araminta brings her hand back to Beulah's wrist in a light sweep and repeats: five times.

4. THE HIPS

BEULAH lies face down.

Araminta kneels beside her (opposite Beulah's mid-thigh) and, spreading thumbs and fingers spider-wise, kneads the hips upward from the legs to the waist-line, using an alternating push-and-tug movement. For the upward push, Araminta flattens her hands and presses with their heels. For the downward pull, Araminta cups her hands slightly and drags at the flesh.

To remove any surplus of cold-cream after the above treatments, use alcohol. Finish this part of the treatment (and the whole massage) by dipping the corner of a rough towel (or better still, a fiber glove) in alcohol and rubbing along the subject's spine, from root to neck, exerting a brisk pressure and being careful to communicate a spiral motion.

It will be found that the last part of the body to respond to the above treatments will be the calves, if they are over-developed or fat. The boss

233

finds that a great percentage of American women have athletic calves, usually acquired during school or college days. A "dancer's calf" is not sightly and Sylvia is besieged by women who want the bulges smoothed out of their legs. Sylvia preaches against excessive exercise for women and recommends high heels. In fact, she abhors the two fads on which so many feminine health-cults are based: mannish sports and low heels. A patient wearing low heels will not be admitted twice to Sylvia's work-room. The boss prescribes the so-called Louis XV heel as the one best suited to the build and locomotive idiosyncrasies of the average female. Conversely, she advises the wearing of low heels, for a short prescribed period (usually a month or two), by women with under-developed calves.

There is nothing more to add to this chapter on exercise and amateur massage. Of the two, the exercises will be found to be the more effective. Admittedly, the massage as described is a weak substitute for treatment by a trained professional.

YOUR MEASUREMENTS

But the described ministrations will do some good
—*and no harm.*

And certainly Beulah and Araminta ought to
be pretty well acquainted by the time the course
is over!

IV

THE CARE OF YOUR SKIN AND HAIR

THE SKIN is a register on which your sins leave their autographs, home addresses and usually a couple of complaints about the management.

It's as difficult to change this record as to kite a check—but it isn't illegal.

Difficult—but not impossible.

Again here we run smack into the diet question at the very outset. If your trouble is a general condition (oiliness or dryness) you'll have to eat your way to happiness. Sweets, starches, the bad habit of "nibbling" between meals; these cause an oily skin. And if your epiderm is brittle and dry,

236

you may be suffering from acidity, a condition
which diet will remedy.

Another factor which affects the skin is
the blood circulation. A sluggish circulation, of
course, can be stimulated by exercise and massage.

We'll go at this subject as systematically as
may be:

1. DRY SKIN

FIRST of all, the boss advises you to avoid soap
and water. Water has become an American fetish.
It is granted miraculous, infallible, all-inclusive
powers of regeneration. It is the cure-all. Well, it
isn't.

Parenthetically, this may be the spot for a
word about bathing. Many have the erroneous notion that a hot bath is relaxing and, seeking an interval of rest and recuperation from the day's
strenuous events, plunge themselves into the boiling vat before the evening's round. They are in
error. A hot bath is highly irritating—the very reverse of relaxing. It is the cold bath that is resting.

Cold baths are used therapeutically to combat insomnia. The cold bath is also a great skin tonic, having a temporarily astringement, or tightening effect on the skin. Therefore, if you must use water, use it cold; at least luke-warm.

After the plunge, take a rough towel (or better, a fiber glove) and rub yourself vigorously for about ten minutes, all over. Your skin will be like velvet.

But, to return to the care of a dry skin—at night use a very thin cream for cleansing. Remove all foreign matter very thoroughly from the surface of the skin. After that, take a piece of absorbent cotton and apply a mild face wash instead of soap and water. Wipe away the face wash with a soft cloth. Follow this with a feeding cream, patted gently all over the face; *not* rubbed in. Pat until you feel the tingle of blood rising to the surface. Leave it on for at least a half hour. If you have a husband or better reason for wanting to be presentable at a late hour, remove as much of the cream as you wish. Enough to feed the pores through the night will escape the removing process.

In the morning take your face wash, lave the face thoroughly and dry with a soft towel. You will have a good astringent lotion. Pat it in gently and use it as the powder base.

Dry-skinned people should have a weekly facial massage to stimulate the skin-glands. If you can't afford facials, you can still beat the racket by being especially, jealously, watchful of your diet.

DIET

IN the morning drink a big glass of hot water with the juice of half a lemon in it. (What? Lemon-juice to fight acidity? Strange as it may seem, lemon juice *does* just that!)

For breakfast, zweiback or toasted whole-wheat bread. If you eat bread, let it be at least twenty-four hours old. You may have coffee with skimmed milk.

For the major meals you have a choice of clear broth or any vegetable soup. You may select your menu from the following: lettuce, celery, to-matoes, radishes, ripe olives, yoghurt, cottage cheese. For an entrée: noodles, macaroni or a cereal. All vegetables. Twenty-four hour old bread, toasted. Eat no meat, fish or eggs. For dessert: fruit ices, fruit gelatins, or fresh figs.

An effervescent salt called citro-carbonate is indicated when there is too much acid in the body. However, the continued use of salts, like that of laxatives, is injurious and apt to become habit-forming. Let the use of all medicinal preparations and drugs be purely temporary, to be discontinued the moment the desired effect is at all noticeable. After all, the only reason for taking medicine is the hope and expectation that you'll get well enough not to need it.

2. OILY SKINS

SYLVIA advises a thin cleansing cream for removing makeup and dirt.

People with oily skins are apt to have white-heads under the skin. The best treatment for white-

heads that the boss has been able to find is a simple
one, based on the use of pure Castile-soap lather.
Work up the lather in warm water. Smear it over
the face and neck. Take a very soft face-brush and
work over the lathered surfaces. Remove the lather
with warm water. Promptly douse the skin with
cold or iced water to close the pores. This is done
just before retiring. The principle of the treatment
is entirely mechanical. The warm lather friction
opens the pores: the cold dousing closes them: the
alternating expansion and contraction eventually
dislodges the clogging deposits in the pores. The
morning after this night treatment wipe the face
with a warm damp cloth. Rub the skin with ice.
Use an astringent as powder base.

Many of the troubles ascribed to an "oily
skin" are in truth the result of a certain bad habit
in the use of cosmetics which is common among
women. I refer to the continual powdering of the
face throughout the day, without removing earlier
applications of powder and rouge. The effect of
this continual and unclean dabbing is to work the

241

earlier layers of cosmetics (and the street-dust which accumulates on them) into the pores of the skin. Sylvia recommends that her patients carry a small vial of face lotion and squares of cleansing tissue, to be used for at least a summary cleansing of the face just before every new application of powder is put on. The film actresses in her care are instructed to keep a jar of thin cleansing cream handy on the movie lot and are told to cleanse the face completely between every application of make-up.

DIET

An oily skin is symptomatic of so many different kinds of incorrect eating that the only diet advice to be given is contained in the general dictum: eat right. Your oily skin is the outward sign of some inward wrong. If you examine yourself honestly, if you use your tape-measure to discover wherein you depart, for instance, from your ideal measurements, you will invariably find a bulge or a deficiency somewhere which is another symptom

242

of the condition which is heralded by your oily skin. Finding this more important defect, you will take calisthenic and dietary measures to correct it. And lo, your oily skin is improved in direct ratio to the improvement elsewhere. If you eat at odd hours (especially, late at night) you need look no further for the causes of an oily skin. And if you eat fried foods habitually, you are certainly going to be as greasy as the stuff you take into your system.

3. SKIN DISORDERS

THE boss has accumulated a quantity of recipes and treatments designed to benefit the victims of various kinds of skin and scalp disorders. I put them down in the order in which the old envelopes, calling cards, scraps of wrapping paper—and even one playing card (the ace of diamonds)—on which they have been scribbled come out of the old shoe-box which is their filing-cabinet.

Blackheads—They are caused by the lazy habit of applying new make-up over old. First,

243

stop the bad habit. To get rid of the heads, apply hot steaming towels, until the skin is fever hot. Then, suddenly freeze the skin by clapping on handfuls of crushed ice. The reaction lays the pores open. Using a magnifying mirror, squeeze out the blackheads—*very gently*—and try not to leave an excavation! As soon as *one* blackhead has been successfully bagged, dab all the area around it with an astringent, and quit. Never try for more than one blackhead at a session. A long drawn-out process!

Hives—Invariably traceable to an element of the diet. Temperaments and body chemistries being so different, the oddest and most unsuspected food may be the cause. It may be salt, it may be milk, it may be strawberries; a certain meat, a certain vegetable. Only one thing to do. Settle down to a patient, unrelenting Scotland Yard search for the offender. Choose a diet covering, say, five or six meals. Stick to it for a week. If the hives persist, eliminate *one* element of the daily menu. Wait again. Continue eliminating, changing, keeping a record, until the elimination of some one particular food-product is followed by relief. Thereafter, banish this product and kindred ones from your diet, *forever*. The long process is worth while, as you will probably be free of hives for the rest of your life.

Cold Sores—Not very serious and usually disappear without breaking. But very annoying. If they persist, apply an alum solution. Dissolve a half-teaspoonful of powdered alum in four ounces of hot water. Cool. Apply morning and night.

Sunburn—*Very* serious. A real burn will destroy the brilliance and gloss of the skin forever, the new growth of skin never attaining the beauty of the old growth that was destroyed. While burned, never use water. Wash gently with a 5% solution of bicarbonate of soda.

(One of Sylvia's patients came in one day with a 102 degree fever and a sharp case of sunburn contracted under a patent "violet ray machine." The boss will not permit a client to own one of these machines, which absolutely belong

245

only in a doctor's consulting room, to be used there with scientific knowledge, in stop-watched doses and with a trained nurse attending.)

Chilblains—Contracted usually by children and old people. Caused by poor circulation. Warm baths, woolen underwear, massage twice a week. For the massage, use an ointment mixed of equal parts of turpentine and olive oil.

(The boss has a mental twist which gives her antipathies to people with certain complaints, among which is chilblains. She says she could get up a system of applied industrial psychology based on people's chronic minor ailments. "I'd never hire anybody with chilblains to work for me," she has told me. "That's a complaint of low-energy folks —the type that loves to lie down and take it.")

Warts—Lay off. There are several kinds, and one or two are innocent. But a wart may be fore-runner of skin cancer, and there is no excuse for postponing the visit to the doctor. A wart may also be an indication of a congenital disorder detectable only through blood tests.

Freckles—Personally, the boss sees no reason for quarreling with these innocent variations of the prevailing pigmentation of the skin. But then, she has freckles herself! A certain type of woman who affects an interesting pallor abhors them. Mae Murray never stirred out into summer sunlight without a red-tinted veil over her face. The device works, as it excludes or tempers the sun-rays which stamp the skin with freckles. Once they're acquired, freckles are sometimes hard to get rid of. A peroxide-and-lemon bleach will make them fade, but is dreadfully drying to the skin. After the bleach, use a thin cold cream, and stop washing with water.

Acne (Pimples)—As in the case of hives, traceable solely to an error of diet. Use the same method of hunting down the pimple-producing food-product described under the *Hives* heading.

A formula for Softening Water—If the local water irritates your skin, temper it to your sensitive, inflamed or dried skin by using one of the following softeners:

247

Bicarbonate of Soda ⎱
Borax ⎰ A little less than ½ ounce of either to each gallon of water

Bran   ½ gallon to a tub of water

Starch   ½ pound to a tub of water

The Hair—To shampoo, drench the hair thoroughly with water. Then work up a Castile-soap lather in the hands and rub thoroughly into the scalp. Rinse for five minutes in flowing warm water or in five still waters. A final rinsing of cold water. Rub the hair dry with hot bath towels. Complete the drying in sunlight or with an electric fan before an open fire-place. The commonly used electric hot-air drier is a short-cut and, like most short-cuts, is harmful to the scalp and hair, making the one dry and the other brittle.

When the hair is dry, rub a little sweet almond oil or vaseline into the scalp, parting the hair repeatedly and rubbing in the parts, so that the oil does not spread into the hair.

The hair must not be washed more than twice

248

a month, preferably at much longer intervals. A daily washing is a sure way to ruin. The daily cleansing of hair and scalp is done with brush and comb. The more time you can give to the daily operation, the better. Those who treat their hair tenderly never wash it, but trust to comb and brush entirely. Use a coarse-toothed comb only. Clean and disinfect your combs and brushes with disinfecting soap, alcohol, or diluted ammonia—if possible before every use, at least once a week.

Massaging of the scalp is very beneficial in cases both of excessive oiliness and excessive dryness. Massage upwards and forwards. The same applies to the brushing—upwards and forwards.

WELL, I've come to the end of my rope. If the boss knows much more about the business of getting beautiful and keeping that way, she's been holding out on me. Anyway, what's set down here ought to keep you busy for a while. Too busy? Ah, there's the rub. The eternal question is: shall I go upstairs and pop a pimple or stay down here and cook papa's supper? I can't help you decide the ethical puzzle. For beauty you need time. Time is the most costly thing there is. Even the idlest matron, curled in the lap of luxury, knows something about the price of hours and minutes.

You may throw this book into the ash-can.

Because you may be after something more valuable than beauty.

If you have found anything answering that description, I'd like to hear about it. Give a girl a tip. I'm not so hot on looks—and I'm looking for an opening.